Reflections
on
Marriage
and
Spiritual Growth

Reflections on Marriage and Spiritual Growth

Edited by
ANDREW J. WEAVER
and
CAROLYN L. STAPLETON

Abingdon Press
Nashville

REFLECTIONS ON MARRIAGE AND SPIRITUAL GROWTH

Copyright © 2003 by Abingdon Press

This book is printed on acid-free paper.

Library of Congress Cataloging-in-Publication Data

Reflections on marriage and spiritual growth / edited by Andrew J. Weaver and Carolyn L. Stapleton.
  p. cm.
Includes bibliographical references.
  ISBN 0-687-08543-8 (alk. paper)
  1. Marriage—Religious aspects—Christianity. I. Weaver, Andrew J., 1947–II. Stapleton, Carolyn L., 1947–

BV835 .R44 2003
248.8'44—dc21

2002013998

All scripture quotations unless noted otherwise are taken from the *New Revised Standard Version of the Bible,* copyright © 1989, by the Division of Christian Education of the National Council of the Churches of Christ in the United States of America. Used by permission. All rights reserved.

Scripture quotations marked RSV are taken from the *Revised Standard Version of the Bible,* copyright © 1946, 1952, 1971 by the Division of Christian Education of the National Council of the Churches of Christ in the United States of America. Used by permission. All rights reserved.

Scripture quotations marked NIV are taken from the HOLY BIBLE: NEW INTERNA-TIONAL VERSION®. Copyright © 1973, 1978, 1984 by the International Bible Society. Used by permission of Zondervan Publishing House. All rights reserved.

Scripture quotations marked TEV are taken from the Today's English Version—Second Edition. Copyright © 1992 by American Bible Society. Used by permission.

03 04 05 06 07 08 09 10 11 12—10 9 8 7 6 5 4 3 2 1

MANUFACTURED IN THE UNITED STATES OF AMERICA

To
Janet and Sammy
John and Doris
with aloha

"Marriage is the ultimate spiritual journey."

—Joseph Campbell interviewed by Bill Moyers in *The Power of Myth*
(New York: Anchor Books, 1991)

Contents

Acknowledgments

We are thankful to Bishop Joel N. Martinez of the San Antonio Area of The United Methodist Church and President of the General Board of Global Ministries of The United Methodist Church for writing the foreword for this volume. A portion of the proceeds from this book will go to the United Methodist Committee on Relief for the AIDS Orphan Trust, a ministry in Africa.

We are also appreciative of the assistance of Julia Oppenheimer, Michelle Hussey, and Lavada Lindsey for their help in preparing the manuscript.

Foreword

The stories shared in this book are not prescriptions for success but invitations to reflection on our own journey in the marriage covenant. Bookstores, libraries, and the Internet abound with "how to" books about relationships and marriage. Far from claiming prescriptive status, these couples write about their journey in marriage with humility born of the twin experiences of human frailty and unbounded grace.

These people are interesting people! After reading their accounts, you will want to meet them and have them tell you more about themselves, their family, and their faith. We are able to see glimpses of lifelong journeys—snapshots of their lives. While each story is different, the theme that unites is the sustaining power of Christian faith learned, lived, and practiced in the intimacy of marriage. I am convinced, in this regard, that the journey into the deepest intimacy with another person is God's invitation into self-revelation. In that self-revelation, we are set free to love and be loved, to give and receive, to flourish and grow as God's children.

In my reading and reflection on these stories, I noted several recurring ideas that bear further, brief comment. One has to do with listening. To listen actively to another person is probably the most difficult interpersonal skill to learn. To listen well is to love well. To listen well is to express the deepest respect. The stories you will find here are, in a variety of ways, about practicing listening even in the most difficult moments of the journey. And it means a listening to the words and the feelings, to the spoken and the unspoken. In a word, it means the whole person listening with his or her whole being to the other whole person. Not easy, but rewarding.

Another has to do with change. Marriage cannot work between people who see themselves as either immovable objects or irresistible forces. The couples who tell their stories in this collection may have had moments when one or both felt or saw themselves in that way. But it did not become a life pattern. The theme that explains these marriages is change, adaptation, and growth. These persons have been willing to give themselves permission to rethink, to change directions, to incorporate new learning and insights. They honor and appreciate their partner's gift to them. They offer theirs as well. The two are

13

enriched by the other's generosity. Inspired by their faith, they risk change and love each other in the midst of it.

A third idea is that of trust. These couples understand not only how essential it is, but also how it must be tended. Trust is a plant that needs constant nourishment. It needs cultivation. Marriage is a journey of husband and wife. It is also a journey of trust and mutual respect. As the journey lengthens, the need for trust and mutual respect grows. The persons who have shared their stories have learned this and their faith has been the nourishing soil.

My wife, Raquel, and I have been married for forty-one years. We have not journeyed alone. Our birth families, our family of faith, and our children have been companions on the way. Ministry has been a particularly shared experience. As baptized people, we have accepted Christ's commission to share in the living and telling of the gospel. Like the couples in the stories collected in this book, our marriage journey is inseparable from our spiritual journey. We are overwhelmed with thanksgiving for God's care and mercy each day. Since none of us can predict the last day of our human journey, we both have come to understand that the destination is the journey itself. While on the way, we have discovered home: with each other, with our family, with the family of faith, and with all of God's children.

I commend these stories of couples who have grown in love and understanding in faith and hope as they have journeyed into the mystery of that love, which 1 Corinthians 13:8 tells us, never ends.

Bishop Joel N. Martinez
San Antonio Area
The United Methodist Church

Introduction

Do Couples Who Pray Together Stay Together?

Andrew J. Weaver and Carolyn L. Stapleton

In the United States, young couples marrying for the first time have about a 40 to 50 percent chance of divorcing—one of the most stressful events that a person can experience (Kitson and Morgan, 1990). Marital difficulties and divorce present major risk factors for emotional problems in both children and adults. And the number of youngsters affected by divorce has increased dramatically—nearly one in three born in the 1990s will experience the disruption of divorce, as compared to one in ten in 1970 (Norton and Miller, 1992). About one-third of the children of divorce will experience long-term emotional difficulties (Kurtz, 1994). Can religious involvement improve the odds of marital stability and satisfaction? After recently reviewing over eight hundred articles in six major marriage and family journals, researchers found that the answer to these questions for many couples is yes (Weaver, Samford, Morgan, Larson, Koenig, and Flannelly, 2002)!

There is increasing evidence that for a significant number of people, commitment to a nurturing faith community enhances family life and marital stability. Greater religious involvement has been associated with marriage satisfaction and positive adjustment to marriage in studies using large nationally representative populations (Bock and Radelet, 1988; Glenn and Weaver, 1978; Kunz and Albrecht, 1977; Wilson and Musick, 1996). In a national survey of 4,587 married couples, results showed that when spouses attended church or synagogue together regularly, they had the lowest risk of divorce among all married groups (Call and Heaton, 1997). This study suggested that shared participation in a faith community gives a couple a sense of purpose and mutual values, which increases family commitment and enhances an integrated social network of relatives and friends.

A separate twelve-year longitudinal study using a national sample of married persons found a consistently negative association between divorce and marriage difficulties and frequency of church or synagogue attendance (Amato and Rogers, 1997). Married couples who participate in worship reported lower levels of problems such as jealousy, moodiness, infidelity, irritating habits, spending money foolishly, and alcohol and drug use than couples who do not participate in worship. The researchers suggest that couples who practice their faith may internalize behavioral norms that are taught in the religious community that are consistent with marital commitment.

In a comprehensive study of married couples living in a Midwestern city, researchers investigated the relationship between joint religious activities and faith-based belief about marriage with their marital functioning (Mahoney et al., 1999). They found that greater involvement in joint religious activities and increased perceptions of marriage as having a spiritual dimension were linked to better functioning in several nonreligious aspects of marital life. The data demonstrated a consistent positive relationship between couples incorporating religious beliefs and practices into their marriage with marital satisfaction, collaboration, and few marital conflicts. This study strongly supports the efficacious effects of public and private faith involvement for couples.

Religious commitment is a consistent predictor of long-term marriage (Kaslow and Robison, 1996). Couples who had been married for more than thirty years indicated that religion figured prominently in their lives. Many spoke of the spiritual support and comfort that faith offered during difficult times. Their religious beliefs also encouraged commitment through the value placed on the marital bond in their faith's teachings (Robinson and Blanton, 1993).

Another study surveyed couples who had long-term marriages of between twenty-five and forty-six years (Kaslow and Robison, 1996). They were given forty-four possible answers to the question of why they stayed together "during difficult times in their marriage." The fifth most common choice (selected by about one in three) was that their commitment was based upon their "religious convictions about the sanctity of marriage." Nearly two in three of the couples indicated that similar religious beliefs had been essential to their marital satisfaction. Studies in the U.S. and Europe have found that shared faith and values are important predictors of stable, satisfying marriages (Kaslow and Robison, 1996).

At a time of widespread concern about the demise of the family, it is important that we understand more about what factors support marriage and family life. Couples are more likely to thrive when they are supported by communities of people committed to marriages. Churches and synagogues are our society's most common institutions that have both a vested interest in preventing marital breakdown and the capability to deliver counseling and education. If active involvement in faith communities can increase marital commitment and serve as a deterrent to instability and divorce, it is important that people of faith understand this.

Reflections on Marriage and Spiritual Growth provides committed couples from within the Roman Catholic and Protestant communities with an opportunity to reflect on marriage as a part of their faith journey and to share their insights with others. They offer lessons and wisdom about married life from their experience of living in a commitment of faith over many years. They share their struggles and satisfactions in the context of their faith. The couples responded to such questions as: How has marriage led to a deeper and enriched faith? How has Christianity been important at different stages in their marriage? What type of spiritual support has Christian faith and community offered during difficult times in their married life? How are marriage and the spiritual journey related? What direction might be offered to those who are struggling in their marriage? What counsel does our Christian heritage offer to married couples? How has faith affected marital intimacy, acceptance, and mutual respect?

We believe that readers will be as moved as we have been by these essays. The authors have been extremely generous in sharing their experiences and some of the intimate details of their marriages. The results are a blessing.

Resources

Amato, P. R., and Rogers, S. J. (1997). A longitudinal study of marital problems and subsequent divorce. *Journal of Marriage and the Family, 59,* 612-24.

Bock, E. W., and Radelet, M. L. (1988). The marital integration of religious independents: A reevaluation of its significance. *Review of Religious Research, 29,* 228-41.

Call, V. R., and Heaton, T. B. (1997). Religious influence on marital stability. *Journal for the Scientific Study of Religion, 36*(3), 382-92.

Glenn, N. D., and Weaver, C. N. (1978). A multivariate, multisurvey study of marital happiness. *Journal of Marriage and the Family, 40,* 269-82.

Kaslow, F., and Robison, J. A. (1996). Long-term satisfying marriages: Perceptions of contributing factors. *The American Journal of Family Therapy*, 24(2), 153-70.

Kitson, G. C., and Morgan, L. A. (1990). The multiple consequences of divorce: A decade of review. *Journal of Marriage and Family*, 52, 913-24.

Kunz, P. R., and Albrecht, S. L. (1977). Religion, marital happiness, and divorce. *International Journal of Sociology and the Family*, 7, 227-32.

Kurtz, L. (1994). Psychosocial coping resources in elementary school-age children of divorce. *American Journal of Orthopsychiatry*, 64, 554-63.

Mahoney, A., Pargament, K. I., Jewell, T., Swank, A. B., Scott, E., Emery, E., and Rye, M. (1999). Marriage and the spiritual realm: The role of proximal and distal religious constructs in marital functioning. *Journal of Family Psychology*, 13(3), 321-38.

Norton, A. J., and Miller, L. F. (1992). *Marriage, Divorce, and Remarriage in the 1990s: U.S. Bureau of the Census, Current Population Reports, Series P-23, No. 180.* Washington, D.C.: U.S. Government Printing Office.

Robinson, L. C., and Blanton, P. W. (1993). Marital strengths in enduring marriages. *Family Relations*, 42, 38-45.

Wilson, J., and Musick, M. (1996). Religion and marital dependency. *Journal for the Scientific Study of Religion*, 35, 30-40.

Weaver, A. J., Samford, J. A., Morgan, V., Larson, D. B., Koenig, H. G., and Flannelly, K. J. (2002). A systematic review of research on religious variables in six primary marriage and family journals: 1995–1999. *American Journal of Family Therapy*, 30, 293-309.

Andrew J. Weaver, Ph.D., is a United Methodist minister and a clinical psychologist. He is Director of Research for the HealthCare Chaplaincy in New York City and coauthor of *Counseling Troubled Older Adults* (Nashville: Abingdon Press, 1997), *Counseling Troubled Teens and Their Families* (Nashville: Abingdon Press, 1999) and *Counseling Families Across the Stages of Life* (Nashville: Abingdon Press, 2002).

Carolyn L. Stapleton, D.Min., is a United Methodist minister and an attorney and is married to Andrew J. Weaver. She is Associate Pastor of Chinese United Methodist Church in New York City and the author of a number of articles.

1

A Love for All Time

Cynthia and John Astle

The voice of our teenage son, Sean, rang out strongly over the worshipers at Casa View United Methodist Church in Dallas:

> Love is patient; love is kind; love is not envious or boastful or arrogant or rude. It does not insist on its own way; it is not irritable or resentful....

Our son read this passage from 1 Corinthians 13:4-8*a* at the conclusion of worship on Sunday, March 25, 2001. The occasion was the renewal of our vows on our twenty-fifth wedding anniversary.

Looking back over our marriage, we found these words to be the best example of the central role that our Christian faith has played in our partnership. This passage became the basis for the following dialogue and interview that reflects our partnership and what our partnership has wrought in us individually.

1. Love is patient.

Cynthia: I am not always a patient person. That is why I value John's patience so much, especially as it has evolved in coping with my mental illness of depression.

I developed clinical depression after two surgeries for endometriosis in 1990 and 1992. Irritability and anger are two symptoms that signal when I am having a depressive episode. John has come to recognize that these symptoms are not character flaws but evidence of illness. His infinite patience when these episodes occur—thankfully far apart these days—is one of the gifts of his love. He gives me an example to follow.

John: Cynthia has almost always been patient with my character flaws. I am very nearly a workaholic, so I have not always been punctual in getting home after work, and I often bring work home with me. I know there are times when she has waited patiently for me, and I am always very glad to see her and to have those few moments late at night before she goes to sleep. Some of my worst guilt occurs when I finally get home and find she has already fallen asleep.

2. Love is kind.

Cynthia: John is one of the kindest people I know, but he is kind in a way that does not rob a person of dignity. I have learned much about the Christian virtue of kindness, which I see as the first element of hospitality, from watching my husband behave kindly toward others.

John: We are kind to each other. In being so, we are able to extend kindness to others. Early in our marriage, my youngest brother was having problems at home and came to live with us for a period. I know that this was a bit of a strain on our marriage, but Cynthia accepted this and helped make a difference in my brother's life. Later, my brother divorced and was in a custody battle for his son. Cynthia was right by my side in offering him support, a place to stay, and, ultimately, a home for him and his son. This kindness that Cynthia embodies is an inspiration to me and one of the reasons I love her so.

3. Love is not envious.

Cynthia: It takes someone without envy to withstand the private shocks of a spouse's public career. That is how John has responded to my far-flung ministry as a religion communicator since I joined the *United Methodist Reporter* in 1988. John has seen me off on trips to Europe, the Middle East, Asia, South Africa, and the Caribbean, not to mention just about every major U.S. city. Not once has he complained.

It is ironic how things turned out because when we were dating in high school, John was the one who loved to travel, who was considering a career in ordained ministry. In fact, our first date was marked by our first prayer together, and our second date marked our first kiss.

Coming out of that background, I think that only a man without envy would allow his wife to traipse all over the world by herself as a scribe for God.

John: Allow? I have never been able to understand the whole concept of any person, husband *or* wife, allowing or disallowing a facet of his or her spouse's being. Cynthia is not "allowed" to travel the globe—she travels the globe. That is her job, and I believe she enjoys it. What possible right would I have to deny her that? She is wrong on one point, though. I *am* envious of her travels. I would not mind going to half the places she has been! But, alas, I am a bit of a private person. Cynthia enjoys a more public arena. Despite this, we each do what we do, give each other space when needed, and try always to be there when the time calls for togetherness. I do not believe we are envious of each other's achievements because we are able to share in each other's accomplishments.

4. Love is not boastful.

Cynthia: This one is easy now, but it grows out of one of our worst experiences together. We had been married about three years when things got really bad in our relationship, mainly from a breakdown in communication. We separated—for four days! When we reconciled and agreed to seek counseling together, we became "we" again.

Since then, I have come to think of us like the Trinity, with God as our third partner. Each of us has a separate personality and operates independently at times, but when we come together in our relationship, interacting, we come fully to life. The wealth of this love—the fullness of our individuality that somehow becomes more full in relationship—simply leaves no room for boasting.

John: Yes, we have had our "not-so-good" times, but we have always risen above them. We still hold hands when we walk around a lake. I guess, in a way, we do boast of our love, but it is in a more subtle, nonboastful way. We are still deeply in love and happy because of this. We may be boastful in the truly innocent ways that we may exhibit our love.

5. Love is not arrogant or rude.

Cynthia: We tease each other mercilessly. Sometimes our whole house rocks with laughter. But our humor is never hurtful because we value each other so much.

Arrogance or rudeness has always seemed like a power play to me, an effort to dominate another person by refusing to exhibit the simple courtesy due another human created in God's image. If anything, John and I—and our son, Sean, too—are more courteous with one another and with strangers because we know so much mutual love and respect. At times our respect for one another is comical, like the old joke about the two Frenchmen, Alphonse and Gaston, trying to outdo each other with politeness: "After you, Alphonse. No, Gaston, after you."

John: I have been called cynical and sarcastic. Cynthia recently got me a T-shirt with the slogan: "Sarcasm, just another service we offer." Honestly, I do not mean to be patently sarcastic. I just sometimes see what I feel is a humorous twist to a situation or someone's actions. Unfortunately, I have to admit my response to what I see as a fallacy in a particular situation may be taken as arrogant or rude.

As Cynthia mentions, we as a family have come to understand, and I believe value, this type of interplay as a method of understanding others' perspectives.

6. Love does not insist on its own way.

Cynthia: This is where I sometimes err in the wrong direction. Because I have spent so much time alone on the road, I fear being selfish when I am around other people, so I sometimes neglect my own needs. It has taken me many years of prayer, contemplation, study, and negotiation to learn the difference between selfish insistence that ignores another's needs and mutual fulfillment that benefits the individuals and their relationship. Sometimes I still seek John's permission for something that I have every right to do on my own. Learning to be my own person, to fulfill God's plan for me, is very different from insisting on getting my own way all the time, which is not healthy for anyone.

John: I tend to be a bit selfish. I really try not to be, but I just want to have it my way! We are all made in God's image and should all have the ability to give, as well as receive. This is an area where Cynthia has been a great help to me. She has shown me the joy of giving of herself when I am in need. I am learning, but I still have a way to go.

7. Love is not irritable or resentful.

Cynthia: Oh, guilty, guilty! This is one area where I am still "going on to perfection," as John Wesley would say. Somehow it is easier for John and me to be apart when I am out of town on assignment than it is to bear long hours when we are both at home. John has a very strong work ethic and is a night person to boot, which combine for some very late nights. Sometimes I resent the long hours, much as I try not to, then I feel guilty and try to make up for my bad attitude.

John: Yes, I can be resentful and irritable, but it's not one of my major flaws. I do understand Cynthia's angst at my long hours and late nights. I hope that the time we have together becomes that much more valuable, but I know that time apart can never be made up. Often, what happens, Cynthia will try to make up for her bad attitude toward my late hours, I will try to make up for my late hours, and we enjoy each other's company that much more!

8. Love does not rejoice in wrongdoing but rejoices in the truth.

Cynthia: One of my proudest times was when John chaired the voters' committee that worked to hold an election to recall a city councilman in Florida. The man used a "temporary insanity" defense to beat a charge of shoplifting. He said he was diagnosed with the beginning stage of dementia, possibly Alzheimer's Disease. When asked if he thought his condition affected his competence to serve in public office, the man stated, "I don't see why it should."

Well, we were not the only voters in our town who were outraged by this episode. When it became apparent that there were many citizens willing to exercise their right to stage a recall election, John agreed to chair the committee.

It took four months to gain enough verified voters' signatures to authorize the recall election and another five months to set it up, including time to defend against the councilman's lawsuits to stop the election. John went on temporary part-time status at work to be available to gather signatures, canvass neighborhoods, research state election law, appear on television, and go to court representing the citizens' committee. We received harassing telephone calls and insulting letters, got snubbed by some longtime business associates, and even received threats of physical harm.

When the election was held, the people voted 8 to 1 to remove the councilman from office for incompetence. The result was gratifying, but the election itself was even more satisfying, knowing that we had played a role in securing such a basic right of government for our neighbors and ourselves. John stood up for what was right. I was and am enormously proud to be the wife of a man who displayed such personal and civic integrity.

John: On a different note: We both have been guilty of some "wrongdoing" in our relationship. We realized the truth is, we love each other and in that we rejoice, and, thank God, we are still together!

9. Love bears all things, believes all things, hopes all things, endures all things.

Cynthia: There has been much to bear in our lives individually and together. I have had a lot of ill health, including thyroid cancer in 1997, that we have struggled through together. We have had family crises, such as the suicide of John's father in 1984 and the recent serious illnesses of my mother that have kept me traveling between Texas and Florida. We have struggled with our financial status and debt burden as much as any other "baby boomer" couple. Since we are both eldest children, John and I have often put our own dreams—such as gaining more higher education—on hold so that we could care for our extended family.

Yet the longer we live together, the more that we meet experiences like these together, the more joy I find in our journey. We remain distinct individuals with different gifts and graces, with likes and dislikes that the other must "bear" or "endure," but our companionship supplies much hope. I cannot imagine going through life without my husband.

John: Nor I without Cynthia.

10. Love never dies.

Cynthia: Whenever I think of "never dying love," I think of John's telephone calls.

When we were high school sweethearts, we talked on the telephone every day, even when we had just been on the school bus together! Now, with our hectic schedules, we keep our love alive through telephone calls.

John usually calls me in late mornings when he arrives at his printing office. I always find myself smiling into the telephone when I hear his voice. We rarely talk more than three minutes, but we say so much in that short time. "Are you OK?" "I'm here for you." "I'm thinking of you." "You're precious to me." "Whatever the world might say about you, remember that I love you!"

These phone calls, to me, are the ministry of Christian presence between husband and wife. They reassure me that I do not face the demands of my life alone. They remind me, too, that Christ is present with me through many people, especially through my beloved husband, and that I can be the presence of Christ for him amid the challenges he faces.

John: It is our never-dying love that keeps me going every day. Cynthia personifies Christ for me in a very real manner. She is always there for me, accepts me as I am, loves me, is ready to forgive me, is an example to me. We find Christ when we look for him, and I have found Christ in Cynthia.

2

Married Couples Make the Best Peaceful Wrecks

Joseph and Sally Cunneen

It's hard for me to talk about marriage as a subject distinct from the rest of my life since I've been married to Sally McDevitt for more than two-thirds of my seventy-eight years. It is theoretically possible that I might have become a more mature Christian during the last fifty-one years without being married, but it would have been harder. Even though I still have a lot of growing up to do, marriage has taught me a great deal about what it means to be human.

Christian marriage involves a great act of faith if one makes the marriage promises seriously. Sally and I remember my Uncle Joe, a bachelor, coming up to us at our wedding reception and saying, "You two are so courageous!" We did not know what he was thinking.

My loving parents were devout Catholics, serious about my religious upbringing. Fortunately they did not lecture me, but taught by example, and I grew up believing that all married couples were happy.

Despite my Catholic education—both high school and college at Jesuit institutions—my premarriage spiritual understanding remained rather abstract and individualistic. I was overly confident that mine was the true religion and was quite willing to argue the case with my Protestant and Jewish comrades in the combat engineering battalion in which I served during World War II, but my religious practice was largely formal and did not draw me sufficiently out of myself.

In any case, marriage taught me a great deal about my own limitations; almost inevitably, it compelled me to be less selfish, more concerned with the needs of others. To live up to the impossible promise of Christian marriage ("For better, for worse") requires God's help. Though I was fortunate enough to marry someone with compatible tastes and convictions, there was much I had to learn about her needs, her preferences, and what annoyed her.

I was fortunate in having an older sister who was very bright and helped me see the limitations placed on women. A physics major in college whose professor thought she should go on to graduate school, my sister was socialized into believing that it was high time she found a husband. So she went out with a succession of Fordham boys, tried not to sound too intelligent, and frequently had to stoop since she was fairly tall. But observing her situation did not really prepare me for the radical changes in marriage that have accompanied the enlarged opportunities for women that have emerged in recent years.

The truth is that Sally was a lot less sure that she wanted to get married than I was. What she was sure of was that she wanted to use her intelligence for more than making brownies and cleaning the stove. What she distrusted was the perception of marriage as the culmination of a *passive* passion, something that "happens" to you and that's "bigger than both of you." Both of us had received a large part of our education at the movies and had noticed that the better romantic comedies of the day featured heroines who were as independent as they were good looking. But in the end, Katherine Hepburn or Claudette Colbert had to fit into their predestined role as the "little woman." The advantage we had was that a good deal of our courtship took place in the context of preliminary meetings with like-minded, idealistic graduate students who were hoping to launch an ecumenical quarterly review. I could not help noticing that the group was impressed with Sally's ideas, and the summer before we got married, she was in Europe, arranging with Catholic and Protestant editors for permission to translate articles for the journal that was to be named *Cross Currents*. During the first year of marriage, I thought we had an equitable division of responsibilities: While I was away most of the day teaching, she could work on the magazine in our apartment.

That was the theory, but the quick appearance of three sons changed the scenario. Despite the high drama of those years—Sally's mother died just a week before our first child was born—and the constant demands of infants, the wonder of seeing our own child made it easy to be grateful to a God who allowed us to share in the work of creation. Even fathers can grow in an understanding of self-sacrifice when it is their turn to interrupt their sleep to care for a crying baby.

The overall experience reinforced my conviction that, though unrestricted fertility is neither a realistic nor a Christian ideal in our urban culture, Christian marriage implies an openness to the gift of life. Nevertheless, I now realize that failure to space the births of our children put an unfair burden on Sally. She was a more than capable

27

mother, but she was swamped. I would come home tired from my job as a college teacher, only too glad to stay put. She needed to get out more and restore her sense of self by being with friends, becoming active in the community, perhaps participating in the faculty discussions that I would report on. As she admitted later, she was being swallowed up by home and children.

Nevertheless, our lively children were a large part of our spiritual development, occasions of both joy and concern. If responsibilities can be more equitably divided, I remain convinced that parenting can be a finishing school for Christian adults; its rewards as well as its sorrows and frustrations impel mothers and fathers to call out for God's help and perhaps to break through to a deeper spirituality. There are special vocations that justify exceptions, but on the whole I believe that couples who decide permanently to avoid having children are making their marriage harder.

The deepest tragedy of our married life was the death of our oldest son when he was only nineteen. Most longtime marriages include comparable heartaches; once again, sheer survival sent us back to God. The experience also highlighted another need of married couples: to have a circle of friends, including some who share their faith commitment. I can still remember the sure, healing instincts of our friends who rallied around us at that moment, preparing a special prayer service, all but physically carrying us when we were close to collapse.

Although husband and wife are to become each other's best friend, their world must not become closed in on itself. Just as a good marriage will welcome children, so it needs a broader network of support—not just in emergencies, but on a regular basis; such friends are opportunities for growth and further self-donation. It was not by accident that when we were exhausted and discouraged, Sally and I instinctively dropped in on a wonderfully generous couple nearby who had nine children, little money, a wonderful sense of humor, and an almost perfect recall of old movies and musicals. Marriage requires intimacy but should be shared in ever-widening circles; in our case, this meant involvement with the Catholic Interracial Council and ecumenical protest against the Vietnam War, as well as visiting the feisty but lonely widow in the house down the street. In hindsight, this was clearly a more effective way of communicating real values to our children—and with more long-term effect—than catechetical instruction.

Many Catholics of my generation, brought up before the Second

Vatican Council, needed to learn to praise God with their bodies. Taught that marriage necessarily implied an inferior mode of spiritual life, they could not overcome the sense that the very delightfulness of sex called for a sense of shame rather than gratitude.

Christian marriage is a school of discipline as well as a school of delight. It is only by stages that a couple moves into a new common existence, requiring them to die to the more individualistic way of life they had before.

British Catholic psychiatrist Jack Dominian emphasizes that although sexual intercourse is obviously an intimate bodily encounter, the act involves the whole person. In contrast with casual sexual encounters, when married couples make love, they signify to each other that they recognize, want, and appreciate each other as the most important person in their life; for them, sex has the capacity for a personal affirmation of immense proportions. Since no marriage is without disagreements, lovemaking also facilitates the reconciliation of marriage partners, at the same time that it confirms their sexual identities. It also, Dominian insists, plays a key part in the continuity of our self-acceptance as lovable persons and leads naturally to a desire to express thanksgiving.

Pleasure in sex requires the active participation of partners who know themselves and can communicate with each other about their most intimate physical needs and emotions. But such sexual relationships do not just happen; they are almost coexistent with our development as human beings. Sex is in the head as well as the body, and when these work together in a relationship aimed at the future, all systems are go.

I very much doubt that any formal course can adequately prepare young couples for marriage, especially in a society in which the most powerful means of communication are constantly barraging them with unrealistic and sentimental romanticism and the explicit encouragement of casual sex. But surely the churches ought to be able to provide better support systems than they do at present. It is hazardous to generalize on this subject—some individual parishes and specific dioceses have developed very useful programs—but young Catholics may be especially lacking in role models and down-to-earth advice because we do not have married priests—or female priests, who would also offer an important resource. Of course, there are male celibate priests—in my experience, especially elderly contemplatives—who are able to communicate the authentic sense of joy that should be at the center of Christian married love.

In any case, I am firmly convinced that the laity should overcome their passivity and recognize that it is up to them, not the institutional church, to meet the need for realistic programs of marriage preparation and living out marriage promises. This is confirmed by the history of the Christian Family Movement (CFM), in which small groups of married couples met regularly to share their concerns and offer one another support. The biblical texts to be used for the approaching Sunday liturgy provided a thematic center for discussion, which was led by each couple in turn. According to the slogan of the movement, the couples were to "observe, judge, and act," which meant in practice that the CFM encouraged a move away from a purely individualistic piety and encouraged serious observation of and response to social issues that its members began to recognize. Predictably, this led to cooperative action with other Christians as well as non-Christians in offering responses to everything from the need for teen centers and low-cost housing to the welcoming support of immigrants and refugees.

Unfortunately, the movement foundered in the wake of Pope Paul VI's 1968 encyclical on birth control, *Humanae vitae*, and would now have to be rebuilt almost from scratch. The encyclical was especially disappointing because the tenor of the Second Vatican Council's statements on marriage indicated that significant progress had been made in the hierarchy's understanding of the "ends of marriage," which had traditionally placed almost exclusive emphasis on children. Most CFM members had attempted, often at considerable cost to their marriages, to follow loyally traditional Roman Catholic teaching on birth control and had welcomed the creation of a papal commission to reexamine the issue. CFM's lead couple, Pat and Patty Crowley, played an important role in these deliberations by presenting the results of an international survey conducted among CFM members, which included the sometimes agonizing stories of these extremely loyal Catholics and helped shift attitudes among bishops and theologians on the commission. When Pope Paul VI ignored the recommendations of the commission he had created, the repercussions were dramatic— and are felt to this day. It would be hard to assess the degree of alienation from the institutional church this has caused, but it is safe to say that the majority of married Catholics in the West have rejected Paul VI's teaching in this area and its repetition by the present pontiff.

To expect that marriage will simply be a continuation of courtship and honeymoon is obviously naïve, but I am not calling for an acceptance of mediocrity when I insist that survival may well offer deeper pleasures. Teenagers and the young married may not realize how satisfying—and even sexy—a retired couple's afternoon trip to the local coffee shop can be. Having overcome earlier misunderstandings, they may well have entered a new stage of satisfaction; just being together, sharing a few quiet minutes, can become an ongoing reward. One may have become somewhat infirm; in any case, they cannot help but be aware that they may lose their partner and have to go on alone. This moves them to a greater awareness of the source of Christian hope and makes it easier to fulfill the spiritual imperative to "live in the now." Grateful for each hour together, they smile at the young mothers and fathers proudly wheeling baby carriages and want to share their memories with old friends. They fall into routines, but not a rut: The husband improves as a back-rubber; the wife who used to resent making meals begins to experiment with herbs she had never tried before. She may even enjoy drifting off to sleep as her husband reads her an old novel.

Sally's long experience teaching at the local community college taught her a lot about the search for identity and brought her to accept a different description of human beings—*vulnerable sharers*. She taught literature courses entitled "Mothering" and "People in Families," where she heard plenty about physical processes and vulnerability, which are as omnipresent as birth and nature. It made her reflect on how in Christian history such reality has often been denigrated, considered of lesser value than clean, intellectual knowing. If wanting to be honest with, and of help to, each other, married partners might well accept vulnerable sharers as a human identity.

Objectively, vulnerable sharers do not look any different from anyone else. Sally showed me some of the personal essays her students turned in that indicated they had achieved it; she became convinced that only as we come to know ourselves as vulnerable sharers in this web of creation do we carry the deep awareness of our varied relationships around with us, motivating us to do what we can to make things right. Only if we feel as well as know our connectedness can we make decisions that are good for ourselves, our partners, and those with whom we minister or live or work.

Vulnerable sharers gradually grow old; it's part of their identity. Then, Sally says, they might look like the couple holding hands on the sofa in Tillie Olsen's story, "Hey Sailor, What Ship?" When their daughter comes home to see them, she lovingly calls them "peaceful wrecks." This part of their identity represents the difficult discipline of physical diminishment that is accomplished by an ever-greater sharing of mind and spirit. It seems like an achievable contemporary form of sanctity for married people—as well as for others. Sally and I are convinced that it is no mean human or religious ambition to become vulnerable sharers and that long-married folks make the best peaceful wrecks.

3

Tied to Be Fit

William A. Ritter
with an epilogue by Kristine Ritter

Scriptures: Genesis 2:18-24; Ecclesiastes 4:9-12

The first time I met Will Willimon was during Parents Weekend at Duke University, 1993. He was reflecting on his ten years as Dean of the Chapel—what he had learned, what he had unlearned, what he had had to relearn—which led him to the subject of weddings. Prior to his arrival at Duke, he had warned his wife that there was no way they could expect to take a summer vacation, given that he would be busy every weekend with brides and grooms. The way he figured it, kids would graduate in the spring and marry in the summer. And, given the beauty of the building, at least some of them would marry at Duke Chapel.

He was dead wrong, of course. That first summer, he performed three student weddings. He could have vacationed every weekend. Today, while Duke Chapel hosts one hundred and twenty-five weddings a year, only a few of them involve Duke students or recent graduates. The chaplain, you see, was locked in the memory of another era—the era when I married my wife and he married his.

Over the last thirty-six years, I have performed sixteen hundred weddings, which has given me one of the better seats from which to observe the ever-changing nuptial parade. Brides and grooms are older now. Wiser, I cannot necessarily say, but definitely older. When I started out, most of them were twenty-two years of age and younger. The average length of courtship was two years—maybe three. They were starting out young. They were starting out poor. But everybody they knew was in the same boat. And if it bothered them, they did not show it.

Today, the average age of my brides is twenty-seven. The grooms are slightly older. The average courtship period is between five and six years. Sixty percent of my couples are living together at the time of the wedding, or have lived together previously. The last teenager I married was ten years ago. All of which interests me. But of more immediate concern is how the "changing scene" has altered my homilies (those short little sermonettes we preachers feel compelled to deliver at weddings, the better to feel that we are honoring our call and earning our honorarium).

Once upon a time, my homiletical sentiments were stern and sober. I reminded everybody that marriage is a serious business and that building a life together requires hard work and discipline. I warned them that marriage asks more of them than has ever been asked before and requires them to go further than they have ever gone before. I told them it was not going to be a bed of roses—moonlight and roses, wine and roses, or beer and pretzels, for that matter. I hammered hard on the anvil of old-fashioned words like "forgiveness," "persistence," and "commitment." In short, I used the six or seven minutes available to me to take the stars out of their eyes and rivet their feet to the ground. And then, with homily complete, I would announce a hymn (presumably something like "Be Strong, We Are Not Here to Play").

Now I am changing my tune. That's because so many brides and grooms are coming to the altar not only knowing that, but also worrying about that. They expect marriage to be difficult and fear that it may be impossible. So I find myself looking for ways to say: "Hey, in the name of Jesus Christ, go for it. You can do it. Sure, it's gonna be hard. But it's also gonna be good. The outcome will be worth the effort. Marriage is a great thing. It's a wonderful step you're taking. We couldn't be happier for you."

This is the reason I resonated to a wedding homily I heard a colleague deliver on the biblical image of the three-strand cord (Ecclesiastes 4:9-12). So I found the text, went to work on the text, wrestled mightily with the text, fell just a little in love with the text, before tossing the words of the text in the air so that they came down and organized themselves under the title "Tied to Be Fit." For that's what the text says. It says that two will be better than one; three, better than two; and multiple-braided cords, stronger than cords of a single braid. It promises that a certain "fitness" will follow when one becomes two—singular becomes plural—and soloists decide to become halves of a duet (or thirds of a trio).

Ponder the text, beginning with the blunt assertion that "two are better than one," and concluding with the oft-quoted aphorism, "a threefold cord is not quickly broken."

Where do we read it? In the book of Ecclesiastes, that's where we read it. And when can we date it? Relatively late in Old Testament history (about 300 B.C.), that's when we can date it. And who wrote it? Darned if anyone knows. All we know is that King Solomon did not write it, even though the first few words of the first chapter of Ecclesiastes suggest that he did. Trust me, he did not.

As I have often suggested to skeptical congregations, the book of Ecclesiastes is a strange collection of stuff—always realistic, seldom optimistic, occasionally pessimistic, and (for those chemically or temperamentally tilted toward the blues) more than a little depressing. Yet I, for one, like its emphasis on extracting life's sweetness wherever one happens to find it. Ecclesiastes never ventures very far from the idea that life is a tough proposition. But the author says it is even tougher for those who go it alone. This leads to the statement that "two are better than one," which sounds nice when read at a wedding. But it was not written for a wedding. And there is no evidence that the author had marriage in mind when putting pen to parchment. So who are the "two" referenced in this writing?

Scholars speculate. I have read several. Few agree. The "two" could be two friends, two siblings, two coworkers, two citizens, or two of anything. The language is pretty generic. The author is talking about the advantages of pairing up, teaming up, matching up. But since the language does not exclude marriage—and since there is a reference to keeping warm by lying down together—I am going to "hunch" that marriage is at least in the back of the author's mind, the better to move it to the front of mine.

"Two are better than one." I'll buy that, even though I face a danger in saying that. For I carry out my ministry amidst a whole lot of "ones"—some of whom have never been "twos," some of whom used to be "twos," some of whom would give their eyeteeth to be "twos," and some of whom have no interest whatsoever in becoming "twos." And then there are the "twos" who secretly harbor a desire to be "ones," figuring that "two" is not nearly what it is cracked up to be if it means being "two with you." If any of that describes you, let me tell you that I hear you, believe you, feel with you, and will, to the degree it is pastorally possible, be there for you. I am very much aware that "one is a whole number." And I believe that the sanctuary ought to be one of those places where it is perfectly acceptable to say to the head waiter upon entering, "Pew for one, please."

But I have this text to deal with, including my belief that there is truth to be gleaned from it—assuming I am clever enough to find it, bold enough to say it, and you are open enough to hear it. "Two are better than one," the author says. "Why?" you ask. "Four reasons," is the answer.

First, "two are better than one" because they have a good return for their work. I suspect that this reflected an agricultural era when one extra body meant two extra hands, therefore doubling the amount that could be planted, picked, served, or sold. I remember what people used to say about employing junior high boys; one boy is one boy, two boys are half a boy, and three boys are no boy at all. But this is not generally true of adults. Two adults tend to work harder and produce more. One of the delightful things we are learning in today's marital culture is that it does not really matter who does what work—only that shared work feels better and yields more.

Here, let me take a moment and talk about work that is done alongside my work (intimately adjacent to my work). Twenty-five years ago, it became increasingly fashionable for persons married to clergy to differentiate themselves from the work of clergy. "We are clergy spouses," they said. "We are not clergy assistants. Therefore, do not expect us to play the pianos nobody else wants to play, run the programs nobody else wants to run, teach the classes nobody else wants to teach, or sweep the corners nobody else wants to sweep. Congregations are not paying for two. Therefore, congregations have no right to require (or expect) the work of two."

As a speech, it was long overdue and much needed. But speaking for myself, I cannot tell you what a blessing it has been to be married to someone who believes that churches are good places to be, that church people are good people to be with, that the ministry is a calling that spills over and embraces both sides of a marriage, and that there are tasks within the ministry that suit her gifts and that she can and does do (willingly, graciously, and more productively than anybody has reason to require or expect). Her own career notwithstanding, our "two" has been far better than my "one." And my congregations have received incredible returns from our mutuality of effort.

But there are other kinds of returns for the "good work of two"—returns not necessarily measurable in field or marketplace. I am talking about returns related to the raising of children and preparing them for marriages of their own.

We know—and the documentation gets stronger by the day—that intact marriages will produce children who get higher grades, are arrested less often, and remain freer from addictions and pregnancies than kids from marriages that split (or marriages that never occurred in the first place). To be sure, there are exceptions to every rule. And there are some incredible parenting jobs being done solo (or across the divorce divide). But everything I see and read tells me that there are measurable payoffs for kids who grow up in marriages that remain stable. And those payoffs continue in succeeding generations. The single measurable factor that will increase the likelihood that your children will make long-lasting marriages of their own is not their age, their job, their wealth, or their level of education prior to marrying, but whether they come to matrimony with their birth parents still married to each other.

Talking with a woman whose primary complaint about her husband was that "there's just nothing there—he no longer makes me happy," I asked about the impact a divorce might have on her minor children, leading her to ask, "Are you suggesting I should stay in an unhappy marriage just for the sake of my kids?" to which I replied, "I can't answer for you. But knowing what I know about what works for kids, I think I would." Unfortunately, she never came back to hear my speech about who is responsible for whose happiness. But I am not bashful about sharing it. It begins like this:

- My wife is not responsible for my happiness in the marriage.
- My congregation is not responsible for my happiness in the church.
- My bishop is not responsible for my happiness in the ministry.
- My mayor is not responsible for my happiness in the metropolis.
- Nor is my God responsible for my happiness in the universe.

But that's a digression. The point remains that two are better than one because they produce a better return. You can look it up.

Second, they also produce mutual assistance. "If they fall, one will lift up the other." That's what Ecclesiastes 4:10 says, before adding: "Woe to one who is alone and falls." The benefit being described is called "backstopping." Not backstabbing, but backstopping. And it is hard to live without it. If something gets past you or something gets to you, who backs you up? Who picks you up? I have been on the ground (because of both my stupidity and life's cruelty). And I have been reached for. Without such assistance, I might still be lying there.

Third, two are better than one because "if two lie together, they keep warm; but how can one keep warm alone?" Upon reading this, my first thought was of the time (a few winters back) when the power went off. It was off for several days. More to the point, it was off for several nights. Thank God for "bundling." But my second thought concerned the phrase "sleeping together"—and the fact that kids have no way of understanding how much more there is to "sleeping together" than sex. When you sleep with someone for a long time, you know when something hurts her, haunts her, concerns her, or keeps her awake. You know when she has had a bad dream or is in pain. And you also know how incredibly close two people can be in a bed and how incredibly far apart they can be in the same bed.

A friend lost his wife not long ago. She suffered for years before she died—suffered at home, alongside her husband. He has done all right since she died except at night in bed when he wakes up every two hours because months *before* her death, she woke up every two hours. And as he heard her then, he hears her still.

Fourth, two are better than one because "though one might prevail against another, two will withstand one" against all kinds of enemies, including temptation.

Except for the first night, I chose to avoid the comings and strayings on that recent slice of "reality television" known as *Temptation Island*. I did have my secretary download the plot summaries from the Internet so I could keep in touch with everything that happened on the way to the see-all, tell-all finale. Most of you recall the format. Four couples were invited to a beautiful resort on a tropical island. In spite of previous commitments made to each other, the couples agreed to be separated and tempted to see if they would stay or stray. Most of the critics said this was "pure sleaze." But it was more than that. It was incredibly "painful sleaze." People were hurt. Even some of the unattached singles (gorgeous hunks of meat—male and female—who were there to provide the temptation) fell hard for the people they were trying to tempt, which meant that they got bruised (where it did not show). Message being: "Even meat feels." Meanwhile, the producers said: "Trust us. We have taken every precaution against unsafe sex." My friends, when will we ever learn that there has never been a prophylactic big enough to cover the entirety of the human heart?

In summary, two are better than one—for work and warmth, and for assistance and resistance. Followed by "a threefold cord is not quickly broken."

Is the third strand God? The author does not say. So the scholars do not say, either. But I will. Because only when God is factored into the mix does marriage cease being an end in itself. You meet and you date. You court and you mate. You plan five years out. You plan ten years out. You plan thirty years out (fixed or adjustable), all the while asking, "Are we on track with our plan?" and pulse-taking, "Do you think we are doing as well as the other couples we know?" But the key to success may be riding a little looser in the saddle—looking up as well as in—while asking questions like:

- What is God giving to us?
- What is God doing through us?
- What is God asking of us?
- How is God's forgiveness working in us?

I guess I'm lucky. Or blessed. Maybe both. Go back with me to a Friday night dance in the fellowship hall of our church, where we had a great time with a nice mix of kids and adults. There was music by a teen band and a talented DJ. Then the old clock on the wall said that we had reached 9:55—five minutes to closing. Teens, gone home. Families, gone home. Most everybody, gone home. A few of us tidying up in order to go home. The hall was dark, save for those little prism lights swirling on the floor. CDs still spinning. Slow stuff, now. Soft stuff, now. Mellow stuff, now. As the kids might have said, "geezer music."

There were just a few of us left on the floor—five couples, maybe six, none under fifty—along with Anne Murray, the Canadian contralto who was crooning something a little bit this side of "country." It took a while to translate the rhythm from head to feet. What it was, was a waltz (one two three, one two three, one two three). Suddenly the feet remembered, which felt goodly and godly and more than a little romantic. After thirty-five years, can you believe it? Dancing in church, no less. With each other, no less. Close, no less. But what was Anne singing that made it all so special? She was singing, "Could I Have This Dance for the Rest of My Life?"

> Would you be my partner, every night?
> When we're together, it feels so right.

Epilogue: Kristine Ritter

Reflecting on Bill's words, "two are better than one," reminded me of a story I recently read about one of my ancestors. It appears that after the death of her husband, Friedrich Stempel, in 1749, his widow, Ann Stempel, remarried just ten months later. The writer noted that while this might be somewhat disrespectful today, in the eighteenth century, a woman had to marry for her physical survival and the survival of her children. Ann had at least four young children and was pregnant with another when her husband died. Two were not only better in the agricultural age, but economically, two were *essential*. Women today have many more choices, of course. They are quite capable of supporting themselves. They can support their children, if they have any. In fact, they do not even need to be married to *have* those children. The same holds true, of course, for men. They can manage their lives and even adopt children, if they wish.

So why marry at all? Perhaps a recent German study can help us with some answers. This study reported remarkable benefits to husbands who kiss their wives each morning. They have fewer auto accidents and earn 20 to 30 percent more money. In addition, they are sick less and live an average of five years longer. Assuming that it is the close, warm relationship that enables "the kiss" to be something more than the mere pressing of lips, it appears that two are not only better than one, but also can be:

     safer
     richer
     healthier
     and longer living.

I remember my mother saying many years ago, "You've got to be able to work together; a good marriage is teamwork." Industry today is saying two (or four) are better than one. Today, effective teams are seen as a way to make better decisions and produce better quality products at a reasonable cost. Wouldn't this be a great objective for a marriage? Better quality at a reasonable cost? What makes a team successful? Team members who are committed to the goals and objectives of the team.

The data appears to support the premise of "two being better than one," but let me close not with data, but with a word of personal experience—thirty-five years' worth of experience. Through deep pain and great joy, incredible demands on time and strength, memorable experiences and an involvement in something greater than myself, I would not have wanted to do it without my helpmate, soul mate, other half, and best friend. It has demanded all I could give and more, taught me more than I could ever have imagined, and I could never have done it alone.

4

Water into Wine

Robert and Esther Schnase

When the steward tasted the water that had become wine, and did not know where it came from, . . . the steward called the bridegroom and said to him, "Everyone serves the good wine first, and then the inferior wine after the guests have become drunk. But you have kept the good wine until now." Jesus did this, the first of his signs, in Cana of Galilee, and revealed his glory; and his disciples believed in him. (John 2:9-11)

$\mathbf{T}$he dim marquee in front of the hotel announced the occasion for anyone braving the misty Texas hill country night: *"Ron and Lyla Schnase–50th Anniv."* All the leanings of their life were toward simplicity, even in celebration. Pink carnations and baby's breath and tall slender candles softened the modest meeting room where the family and friends gathered. The florals reached across the center of the table in a style recently learned by their daughter-in-law at a church craft class. The crystal cake stand that supported a simple two-layer cake at their wedding fifty years ago served the same purpose again. Near the cake, a framed black and white photo touched up for color displayed a young bright-eyed bride and a slightly self-conscious groom.

The gathering was modest, just over twenty people. The best man from fifty years before was there with his wife, son, and grandson. A sister was there with her husband, son, and grandchildren. And of course, the couple's two sons and daughter along with their families were there. No one wore ties or suits or sequined dresses. After all the poses and photos, everyone sat down to Texas barbecue, potato salad, and iced tea. Waves of laughter would rise and fall with the banter, the teasing, the memories. After dinner the couple opened their gifts with their grandchildren crowding around, pushing and posturing in anticipation.

When everyone settled into their seats again, the lights dimmed, and the screen came alive with images from the past, photos of the couple as children, teenagers, young lovers, newlyweds, parents, grandparents. The collage evoked memories of the sweetness of former times and distant places and long-ago friends. Grandchildren roared at photos of Grandpa as the teenage boxer flexing his muscles. They nearly choked at the sight of their young grandmother standing on her head in a bathing suit at the beach. They were slim and playful and full of youth in the photos and more daring in their day than their children could imagine. There were images of the wedding, the first car, the trailer house in the in-law's driveway, full-time jobs, a child, a move across the country, a new uniform, another child, and a third. There were poignant moments that moistened the eye and tightened the throat when faces of those no longer present appeared on the screen. The images captured the succession of career moves, births, holidays, and houses that have formed their fifty years together, and of the people who have graced their lives.

Just before time to clean the table and put away the gifts, Ron Schnase did something no one expected. The private man who hates to speak in public and who resists anything that focuses attention on himself, arose at his place and asked for attention. What he said took no more than thirty seconds. He thanked all for being there with them to celebrate this occasion. And then he looked across the people sitting at the table and, with a natural and graceful tone, said simply, "This is the best day of my life. There's no place I'd rather be tonight than here, and no people I'd rather be with than the people in this room. Thank you." And then he sat down. In silence, I thought of the significance of my father's words. I sensed the meaning of his words settle into the souls of everyone present.

"There's no place I'd rather be tonight than here, and no people I'd rather be with than the people in this room." It is as if the experiences and people captured in the images of the video, along with the unrecorded events across the years, had led to this moment, and in those simple words he was giving infinite thanks to God for God's kindness in making him the recipient of one of life's greatest gifts.

The disciples of Jesus were perplexed by the sudden and unexpected appearance of such high quality wine at the wedding feast. From ordinary water came extraordinary wine, robust and full and savory. Those who recorded the event describe the change as a sign of God's presence in their midst, as a transformation made possible by the grace of God. Ordinary lives, infused with God's grace, become extraordinarily full of meaning and beauty.

I cannot imagine my parents describing their marriage as a spiritual journey. They did not step into each new day following the guidance

42

and rubric of intentional and explicit spiritual disciplines. They did not use a preprinted map to guide them. And yet they have arrived at a destination that few have achieved. They have not only lived together for fifty years, but also lived their lives together in a way that was satisfying to them.

How many people at any point in their journey together can say with assurance, "There's no place I'd rather be than here, and no one I'd rather be with than the people in this room"? To the contrary, most of us want to move on, move up, move past, move through, or move away from something, somewhere, someone. Whether we experience our current situation as a stage, a phase, a rung on the ladder, a step, or a station, we live with a sense of uneasiness. Our soul's longing rests its hope on what is yet to come.

Stephen Covey reminds us to "begin with the end in mind" (*The Seven Habits of Highly Effective People: Restoring the Character Ethic* [New York: Simon & Schuster, 1989], 95). What is "the end" in marriage? How might we live our lives today, this week, this month, in a manner that takes us to a place many years from now where we can say, "There's no place I'd rather be than here, and no one I'd rather be with than the people in this room"? How do we take ordinary days and live those days so as to experience them in the fullness of time as marked by grace?

The marriage of my parents is not a particularly heroic love story. It is not distinguished by high drama, the overcoming of great obstacles to be together. Theirs is not the story of Romeo and Juliet, full of blind passion or profound conflict. They are not outwardly passionate and romantic like lovers are portrayed in the movies. And they have not understood or interpreted their love in terms of religious motifs and the explicit language of faith. They simply have lived ordinary lives and lived them together for fifty years. At times, I have seen them full of joy and laughter, and at times, I have seen them get along with each other as an act of will.

They have faced the same challenges that most married couples face, if we can trust the photographs and memories. In each marriage is replicated, in small letters, the capital challenges of the centuries, and the history of marriages in many ways consists of successive excursions from the same starting point.

Most people can remember the early blossoming of love, the thrill of a lover's first touch. Sheepishly, most of us can tell of clumsy poems with ungainly phrases and forced rhymes that, despite their literary deficiencies, would bring tears of joy to the recipient's eyes.

Young love, at whatever age, enlivens the soul. Almost everyone recalls the aliveness of receiving a lover's handwritten notes telling of ordinary days, yet these notes are read and reread late into the night and kept in secret places like extraordinary treasures. This part of the journey is marked by exuberance, obsession, excitement, unparalleled joy, and vulnerability.

Following this early period, most marriages go through years of figuring everything out—budgets, jobs, kids, bills, cars, food, getting along. Love requires resilience when life pushes romance through the daily gristmill of practical problems.

As every relationship matures, there is a period of discovering the shadow of the other person, the unattractive habits, the eccentricities and idiosyncrasies, the quirks and mannerisms that make loving a particular person a peculiar and singular task. Some marriages adapt; some break apart. Almost all experience fraying at the edges.

And there is the period of routines, of simply sharing time and space, and, somehow through the succession of days, sharing a life.

These phases do not come with stair-step predictability. We do not graduate from one pattern of relating and then leave it behind. All our ways of relating we carry into successive experiences, bringing all the patterns along into each new day we share. But when we are honest, we are aware that at any particular time the relationship is taking one of these shapes of relating more than the others. Romance, practical necessity, strain, and routine all coexist, but one mood colors a given day more than other moods.

These predictable rises and falls, ruts and reroutes, are just the ordinary stuff of life, common as water. Where is the wine? What does it take to form a life together, to take on the daily task of living together in a way that, in the end, is satisfying?

It takes an enormous amount of *faith* to carry each other from day to day in marriage. The writer of Hebrews reflects on the faith of Abraham, saying, "And he set out, not knowing where he was going" (Hebrews 11:8).

When couples take their wedding vows, they set out with no idea what this journey will require of them, where it will take them, what challenges it will bring, or what resources they will need to keep going. Confidence outweighs uncertainty; promise fortifies against the unforeseeable. They set out not knowing where they are going. Faith takes them to a land where they have never traveled, to face tasks for which they are unprepared. That is the faith marriage takes, each day. That is the faith it takes to bring a child into this world and to take on the joy and task of parenthood. That is the faith required to establish a home, to move into a career, to respond to a vocation, to grow and change and adapt. When we begin a relationship and commit ourselves to it in some form, we have no idea all that will be involved—the difficulties and challenges, the doubts and questions and temptations, the daily grinding down of dream and aspiration by the millstone of routine and commonness and habit and hardship.

We may never learn the formal grammar of the language of faith, and therefore never perceive the explicit gift and task of patience, grace, forgiveness, gentleness, or compassion, but without these constituent features of faith, even if they remain unnamed, it is hard to imagine how two people can take on the daily task of living together.

Abraham and Sarah set out not knowing where they were going. Faith, in marriage, is leaning into the future. It is the core essential consensus that all things—*all things*—are amenable to hope and resolution.

And for us to live together in a way that, in the end, we find satisfying requires the presence of *hope*. Marriage is viewed as a sacrament by the majority of the Christian family, as a means of God's grace. Cynicism is a contradiction of God's grace. Cynicism is the pessimism and doubt and distrust that dries our souls with the astringent lie that nothing matters anyway. In the cynic's idea of marriage, nothing is sacred, and so the joys are illusory and the sorrows are without meaning.

Moses stood before the people of Israel and said, "I have set before you today life and prosperity, death and adversity. . . . Choose life so that you . . . may live" (Deuteronomy 30:15-20). The task becomes to nurture in each other the qualities of hope that allow us to affirm that life is worth living, even when things do not go our own way, and that people are worth loving, even when they disappoint us. At bedrock, hope is the sense that it is all worth it somehow, but maybe in ways we cannot understand or see only in part. The pain and sorrow—the grief and loss, the joy and delight, the successes and failures, the times of closeness and times of distance—are worth it; and somehow there is a thread that weaves all these together into a tapestry that is worth the effort. Hope is not an abstract noun; it is an imperative. It is living toward the completeness we cannot now fully fathom. Hope.

And living together in a way that, in the end, we find satisfying requires *love*. That seems obvious. Maybe what I mean to say is that it requires a new way to look at love if we are to make marriage a spiritual journey.

Too often we look at love as if it is an all-or-nothing proposition. You have it or you don't. It's on or it's off. We're in love or we're not. Or we resort to distinctions between feeling and acting. Is love an emotion or an intention or a set of habits that expresses a commitment?

There is another way to look at marriage and love. For instance, some Christian writers have seen friendship as "a school for love." It is in the intimacy of friendship that we learn to love, that we practice it and perfect it. Our friends sculpt us into who we are. By their love and their influence upon us, as we seek to love them and receive the love they give to us, we become people we never would have become on our own. The most concrete and personal way God reaches down and works on our behalf is through our friends (See Paul J. Wadell, *Friendship and the Moral Life* [Notre Dame: University of Notre Dame Press, 1989]).

Maybe we do well to view marriage as "a school for love." In other words, it is not just that marriage requires some measure of love at the outset, but that marriage serves God's purpose of perfecting us by providing the best and highest arena in which to learn to love. Marriage is a means God uses to form us. It is in the commitment of marriage and through all the experiences of living a life together that we learn how to love. This means we are never perfect in our understanding and practice of forgiveness, patience, compassion, gentleness, but we know we are on our way.

To see marriage as a spiritual journey, as a school for love, allows us to ask ourselves such questions as: Are we doing better now in our practice of forgiveness than we were five years ago? What are we doing to nurture in each other a deeper understanding of patience so that we can do better in five years? Are we doing better at accommodating trivial but annoying idiosyncrasies than we were before? Are we doing better at expressing honest discontent? What have we learned recently in this school about joy? About caring? About tenderness?

Are we living the life that will take us to the place we want to go, so we will be able to say in the fullness of time, "There's no place I'd rather be than here, and nobody I'd rather be with than the people in this room"? To make such a statement is not to presume to have a perfect marriage, or even a perfectly happy marriage. It is to say that one has lived the ordinary days of one's life well enough to see in them a touch of God's extraordinary grace.

When the water becomes wine, the followers of Christ begin to rethink where God is found and how God is known. God is seen in the miraculous appearance of abundance, extravagance, quality, and satisfaction where no one expected to see anything but the ordinary. In the infinite succession of small steps and missteps we take together each day, God schools us in love and infuses our common lives with extraordinary beauty.

5

Marriage on the Road: An Adventure in Faith

John and Carolyn A. Twiname

At this writing, we have been married forty-six years and have three married daughters (one now divorced) and six grandchildren. We have lived in five cities, involving eight moves. It seems to us that faith has evolved to strengthen our marriage through a series of "awakenings" occurring through various challenges. As we look back, each decade represents a phase of spiritual growth in our life together, and with each, we have become closer partners, friends, and lovers. We have God to thank for this growth in experiencing the various facets of love and only wish every marriage could be open to receive these gifts that seem so readily available.

The Foundations of Faith

We grew up with different faith orientations and religious exposure. John's mother played a pump organ in a small Baptist church. After attending a Quaker Sunday school class, John would walk to the Baptist church to sit with his mother through worship, which usually included a "hellfire and brimstone" message. A great imprint was made on him by his maternal grandmother, whose combination of peacefulness and courage through terminal leukemia touched him deeply.

Carolyn attended Sunday school at a local community church, but was jolted when her brother took his life while a freshman at Yale. The minister who conducted the funeral came from another church and spoke about death and eternal life and God's constant presence in such a way that she was drawn to his church. In high school, she sang in the choir there and was nurtured by the religious music and the minister's wisdom and faith.

In Our Twenties (the 1950s): Joining the Foundations

John went to Cornell and, typically intoxicated with college-bred philosophy, began to distance himself from his mother's "old time religion." But even in the midst of distancing was the underlying foundation of idealism, bred by the earlier religious exposure and enhanced by Boy Scout training and the lofty ideals of his fraternity (though more observed in the breach).

Carolyn's faith was further nurtured at Bradford Junior College where Monday evening prayer service and two weekday chapel services were required. To her surprise, she found how much the times of quiet reflection meant in finding balance, hope, and meaning. After transferring to Cornell, she felt lost and alone, missing the community of the smaller college. But one Sunday morning at the college chapel, her weakness was transformed into strength, energy, and new direction when she joined in the rousing hymn (ironically, now almost obsolete) that seemed to infuse her with a personal meaning: "Rise up, O men of God! The church for you doth wait, her strength unequal to her task; rise up, and make her great!" This was but one of successive awakenings for us on the journey of faith.

Our coming together just before John graduated in 1953 was an occasion for much discussion of religion and the meaning of life, as well as the discovery of romantic love. But it was an old-fashioned romance, held together primarily by letters and occasional long-distance phone calls while John fulfilled his two-year obligation in the Army and Carolyn finished college.

In this case, distance made the heart grow fonder. We were married just after the Army discharge and headed for Business School at Harvard. Fortunately, Carolyn could help finance the educational investment by becoming a grade school teacher, though our first daughter was born a semester before graduation. John began his business career by taking a beginning sales territory in Philadelphia for a hospital supply firm, continuing his workaholic habits from school, trying to make a successful start.

If the resurgence of the feminist revolution had occurred earlier, Carolyn might not have been discouraged from reading books about doctors and might have become a physician. As you will see, her dream was later expressed, but in a different profession. However, during the early years, she assumed the traditional role of homemaker, moving to whatever city called John to work.

While immersed in family building, a second daughter was born in

Philadelphia, but it was not easy for Carolyn because there was no built-in community. Moreover, the intensity of John working seven days and nights each week became a "downer" for the whole family, as well as a depleting schedule for him. Life was out of balance. And a workaholic, just like an alcoholic, must come to the realization that he needs help from a higher power.

With Carolyn's guidance, we turned again to the church. And, you could have predicted it; a young couple in their late twenties was just who they wanted to lead their youth group. When it called for discussions of faith, we had to read and think together to try to stay ahead of the kids. Of course, as happens with so many, we were the main beneficiaries. This involvement began to bring life into balance even as it created more work for us. Most important, it moved us to a deeper level of considering what Christian faith is all about.

But sometimes, trying to be religiously faithful does not help engender love. John thought religion was about being good, trying to follow the "What would Jesus do?" injunction. But he saw that his efforts to be "good" were often carried out in a judgmental, condescending manner. The failure he felt in trying to have a loving spirit through self-effort finally left him spiritually exhausted and, he felt, defeated in trying to live "the law of love."

Eventually, on a retreat with the youth group, John felt "brought to his knees" in his predicament. But the gift of "awakening" allowed him to find spiritual renewal in surrendering to God.

In Our Thirties (the 1960s): Nurturing a Faith for the Future

Just after this "conversion" experience, John was promoted back to corporate headquarters in the Chicago area. We were fortunate to end up at a church led by two ministers who challenged our faith while enriching it. It was a critical connection because it was in this community that our third daughter was born, and the struggle over how to raise children became a real test for the marriage. ("You're going to spoil her"; "Raising your voice won't help.") Carolyn played the difficult role of peacemaker as we tried to balance encouragement with behavior control.

A great blessing came when we were encouraged to form a small "koinonia group" for study, prayer, and sharing our faith in open honesty and trust with others. This experience proved formative in nurturing our faith and capacity, both to communicate and to receive deeper love within the family and in all the transactions of life.

As we became involved with the five other couples, we found the key for deepening our own relationship: letting Christ be the "head of our family" and of our marriage. We found that in praying together, silently and out loud, we were drawn into a deeper sense of relatedness based on principles that Jesus had taught and demonstrated. But more important, we were drawn into a personal relationship with God as we imagined Christ as our guide. One of our pastors emphasized the power available, through the Holy Spirit, in this personal relationship with God, and we could feel that empowerment as we yielded our issues, our disagreements, and our questions to this higher power in Christ.

As just one example, John could see the futility in criticizing Carolyn and making her upset. He began to see that his impatience with others was just the projection of his impatience with his own imperfection. He has not yet fully seen the futility in criticizing himself, but at least there is less criticism directed at those around him.

A great spiritual gift was having our church select us to be delegates to a conference at the Ecumenical Institute in Bossey, Switzerland. During Bible study there, with representatives from many countries and other denominations, we were led to a vision of the "Incognito Christ," at work in every person and situation of life. This theological insight, matched with the era's emphasis on "the ministry of the laity," gave us a sense of purpose that inspired many of our involvements in the years ahead.

We were led into political and social activism during the 1960s. Carolyn found her ministry, beyond wife and mother, in developing "start-up" enterprises. She learned the ministry of politics, managing the women's division of the campaign to help a fledgling politician upset the Republican establishment in our district. There was a test of faith in supporting "open housing" in the face of opposing views by community leaders, who included the management of John's company. We felt led to be involved in the inner city's struggle, with Carolyn helping our church get involved by managing an urban-suburban day camp and John leading a project to engage minority community leaders and business and union leaders in dialogue. These Christ-inspired involvements set the stage for the next leap of faith.

In Our Forties (the 1970s): The Future Takes a New Turn

After twelve years with the corporation and becoming a Vice President of Marketing, John received a call from Washington, asking whether he might be interested in serving in the new administration. Leaving the company meant getting off the vertical track to an adventure in horizontal mobility. The social and political issues were important to both of us; we felt prompted by the Spirit to take the leap. This led to John's becoming head of federal welfare and social services in the former Department of Health, Education, and Welfare.

Carolyn became an enthusiastic participant in Washington life. She expanded her volunteer ministry on the Office of Economic Opportunity's Women's Advisory Committee, was a member of the Defense Advisory Committee for Women in the Service, helped start the new Center for Voluntary Action, and was a founding board member forming the University of the District of Columbia. Another of her new "start-ups" was managing a demonstration nutrition program for the elderly. Then she pursued a master's degree in Government and Public Administration to prepare her for a future career and "regular employment."

Exciting as it was to have an opportunity to work for institutional change in Washington, the pressures were enormous. There were not only the difficulties of bringing people of different political persuasions together, but also our three daughters entering adolescence at a time when the Capital was feeling all the rumblings of the uprisings over the Vietnam War—and worse, the emerging influence of a counterculture in sexual behavior, drugs, and general incivility.

Carolyn had found spiritual support in the intimacy of a book group she had founded in our previous home, and she repeated that formula in Washington. But, together, we also turned again to the church for spiritual nurture, though facing our children's resistance to such "old-fashioned" rituals. We rediscovered the power of the small, intimate faith-sharing group. Carolyn's entrepreneurial spirit led a group that had the start-up mission of transforming a somewhat moribund early worship service into a 1960s-type celebration, with guitars, hand-clapping, and liturgical innovations.

It was an enterprise that could involve our whole family and added much vitality to our religious experience. One thing it taught us was the power of praise. The act of praising God in creative ways seemed to result in a greater personal bond with the Divine. But we also discovered that in using more occasions to praise each other, we forged a greater bond in our marriage.

In Our Fifties (the 1980s): A New Adventure of Faith

After two other management roles in government and the private sector, John received a call to move to New York City to become manager of a leading research foundation uncovering causes of, and means of preventing, diseases, primarily cancer and heart disease. Soon after, Carolyn put her new degree to work, becoming regional director of an emergency medical identification program.

After John completed his service at the foundation, he got the idea of a self-awarded sabbatical at Union Theological Seminary, just for a semester, while he considered his next employment. When he found it stimulating, Carolyn encouraged him to continue. She supported him through graduate school just as she had twenty-five years earlier. But her encouragement became a crisis in faith for John: Not feeling a call to ministry, he wondered, *Who will hire me if they find I have a seminary degree?*

The decision was to let it be "an adventure in faith," with the prayer that God would provide some opportunity "as long as it is not a parish, please." (We had viewed in several churches, by now, the pitfalls of parish ministry.)

Indeed, a year later, it was an answer to prayer when John was asked to help find an ordained minister to manage a small Protestant chaplaincy organization very close to our Manhattan neighborhood. When John brought home the organization's brochure, Carolyn read it and wished she could be ordained and apply as its executive. This, truly, might fulfill her dream of becoming a healer. John said he would provide the ordination if she would provide the vision. He took her resume to the search committee and asked it to consider us as a team since we had at times talked about trying to work together "for real" as we had as volunteers, primarily in the church.

The board of The Hospital Chaplaincy accepted the idea, and we became copresidents—our office in an old studio apartment with an administrative assistant, four chaplains, a Clinical Pastoral Education supervisor, and a $90,000 deficit. The five benefiting medical facilities contributed less than 5 percent of the budget. It *was* "an adventure in faith," and we were taught the necessity of trust as the indispensable ingredient of faith.

Forgiveness was another gift that we also had to cultivate with each other because we were almost continually in the same room together, whether at the office or at the apartment. We critiqued each other's written material and negotiated all ideas and plans. We made mistakes

53

right in front of each other, frequently. We learned how to use forgiveness as a preventive form of grace.

Humor was also a spiritual gift for use in these situations. We found that the experience of (and faith in) God's unconditional love gave us great ego strength and self-esteem such that we did not need to kick in ego-defense mechanisms every time we lapsed. When John would catch a mouse in the old office, Carolyn might exclaim, "Good dog!" We could kid and tease each other (and let others, also) and laugh as it helped relieve the tension—not only the tension of our mistakes, but also the stress meeting the payroll.

After surviving the initial crisis, we were further blessed by the new board and staff members, seemingly sent to us by God. These became the small group, or community of faith, that played the role in our faith development as we had experienced in Chicago and Washington. With this support, we determined that the proper way to gain professional recognition in each medical facility was to present ourselves as the provider of health-related pastoral care on a multifaith basis. Before the laughter of doubters died down, we received calls from a rabbi in training to be a Clinical Pastoral Education supervisor and from a highly trained Roman Catholic sister who was interested in a chaplaincy position.

With their employment (trusting that the money could be found) and a couple of trustee additions, The Chaplaincy became the forerunner of the multifaith center for pastoral care, education, and research now representing over thirty faith traditions, training over 250 students annually and serving more than 30 major medical facilities. As our understanding of God grew larger among these colleagues of many faiths, so did our faith in God's more inclusive purposes. The Incognito Christ was at work in a way that raised our vision, lifted our spirit, and buoyed our marriage partnership to a new level.

Though the multifaith ministry meant less time for family, our daughters supported our commitment to it, even referring to it as our "fourth daughter." Our youngest daughter even had her first child blessed in The Chaplaincy's new chapel by us with a Muslim imam, a rabbi, and a Roman Catholic priest.

In Our Sixties (the 1990s): Turning It Over

Seeing an increasing number of patients helped by great chaplains and gifted students, we knew the time had come to find new leadership. We felt we should retreat, perhaps to board positions, so that we could also be more active grandparents. We had already found the need to turn our attention more to family as we suffered through the terminal illnesses of our three remaining parents, who died at the turn of the decade. These encounters with end-of-life passages brought us even closer together, and we were grateful that we had been prepared for them by our work at The Chaplaincy.

The move to get leadership help was implemented at the right time. God answered our prayer by sending a Jesuit priest-psychologist who began as executive vice president, but within two years was able to become the CEO. He took the unusual step of asking us to stay on as members of the team, and, continuing to live in this community of support, we were able to tackle new challenges.

One of our challenges was dealing with the pain of alcoholism in more than one family member. The blessing that came in healing and recovery far outweighed the anguish and brokenness. We experienced the power of "church" in the unconditional acceptance and love of Alcoholics Anonymous and at the "Family Program" at Hazelden. Our granddaughter, age twelve at the time, summed it up by observing, "The whole world should go to Hazelden." Our daughter presented John with a "Turn It Over" keychain to help us remember to keep relearning that need to surrender.

These situations involved new spiritual challenges that made us more dependent on God's guidance and grace. We knew of other parents who became divorced after being intensively together around some extended crisis. In taking care of a third person, they forgot to take care of each other. When God is invited and allowed to be "head of the marriage," though, we found there comes back an enabling energy to love that is far more powerful than the instinct to take out anxieties and frustrations on each other.

We found special meaning in being inspired to conduct weddings together—one couple guiding another couple through the marriage vows. Performing this sacrament together is always a powerful reminder of what God's promises are for those who turn over their marriage to be ruled by the Christ Spirit.

Later in the decade, John found he had to have his mitral heart valve repaired. This invasive procedure, involving sawing the chest open and slicing open the heart, was a great lesson in faith for us as well. John was anxious that his faith would fail him. But happily we learned, in moving toward the operating table, that prayers of gratitude can fill the spiritual space that fear might otherwise occupy. Another "turn it over" experience.

Gratitude is a great gift to cultivate in a marriage, too. Our hearts are being operated on all the time, spiritually and emotionally. Gratitude to God for what we have in each other is a constant prayer to be lifted. It keeps us focused more on each other's strengths than on our limitations.

In Our Late Sixties (The New Century): "The Sign of God Is Being Led Where You Did Not Mean to Go"

At the turn of the millennium, John was called back out of semi-retirement to fill a gap for The Chaplaincy while they recruited an executive vice president. Fortunately, Carolyn helped fill the gap, too, by volunteering to help. After a year of intense work, another unexpected request led to John's assuming an acting senior minister role in a Connecticut church—the very role he had tried to avoid. It was interesting how much we missed each other and the parallel, collaborative roles our relationship had thrived on, although we were both involved in the congregation, with Carolyn serving as a sermon advisor and editor.

Perhaps we will be called to other unexpected roles in the future, but one we are looking forward to is that of spending, together, more time with friends—including our daughters and their families. It is this growing family that represents the best start-up role Carolyn ever took on. The roles have changed, but the victories and defeats, the laughter and the tears, the happiness and heartbreak, still go on.

Our prayers are being answered as our family has grown in faith through life's challenges. Trying to support our family through such times has been instrumental in deepening our own commitment of faith; we have had to "turn it over" rather than try and control. The reward has been the joy that springs up from a foundation of faith.

All these spiritual gifts we have mentioned, to the extent that we have received them "here and there, now and then" (as Paul Tillich and, later, Fred Buechner put it), have flowed when we have placed God first in our marriage and family. Surrender has not felt like servitude; it has felt like liberation to love. Because our ministries have become defined as helping others (and ourselves) toward the wholeness of life that we believe is God's will, it is good to be able to share our own experience of the good news of God's gifts and faith's possibilities for fulfilling the promise of marriage.

6

Two for the Road: Lessons We Have Learned Along the Way

James A. and Marsha Harnish

Genesis 12:1-9; Psalm 16

The continuing joke in our marriage is that, technically speaking, I never asked Marsha to marry me. It was a moonlit night in the bluegrass of Kentucky in the spring of 1968. We had been dating for nearly two years. It was obvious to everyone who knew us that marriage was on the horizon. Neither the anticipated question nor the expected response were in doubt. It was just a matter of doing it. But when the time came, I did not actually speak the words, "Will you marry me?" Instead, I found myself asking, "Will you go to Dallas with me?" My plan, following college graduation, was to do graduate work at Southern Methodist University in Dallas, Texas. Because living together without marriage was not an option for our mutually inbred sense of Christian morality, the meaning of the question was patently obvious. The great good news is that she understood what I meant and said, "Yes!"

The twist in the story is that nearly three decades would pass before either of us would get to Dallas and we have still never been there together! We decided to stay in Kentucky where I would go to seminary and she would teach and earn her master's degree in elementary education. From there, the road led directly to our first pastoral appointment in Florida. It was not until our youngest daughter was serving as a social worker in Dallas that we actually visited the city, and that was on separate trips. As my daughter and I drove by the SMU campus, I told her the story, and we laughed together about the surprising detour her parents' journey had taken.

I guess you could say that from the very beginning of our marriage, we learned that for a United Methodist pastor—at one time known as "traveling preachers"—marriage would involve traveling together with very little ability to predict where the road might lead. In more ways than we could ever have guessed in the beginning, our life together has been a fulfillment of a 1967 movie's theme song that I copied down and sent to her while we were dating. The title of both the song and the film was *Two for the Road*. Although we never saw the movie, the lyrics were deeply embedded into our relationship. The words invited us to "wander through the world" together, collecting memories and living life the way we pleased, with the promise that we would be "two for the road" for a long, long time.

There is solid biblical precedence for a "road trip" understanding of marriage. The story of the covenant begins in Genesis 12, when God says, "Go!" and Abram gets up and goes. Biblically speaking, faith means walking in obedience to the call of God with little or no clarity about exactly where the road will lead, but with absolute trust in the One who is leading the way. Faith is defined by the direction in which our feet are moving. Are we walking in obedience to the call of God, or are we walking away from it?

But Abram did not travel alone. His wife, Sarai, went with him. Biblical faith is not a solitary hike; faith is always walking together in obedience to the call of God. The Genesis writer said, "Abram journeyed on by stages" (Genesis 12:9). Along the way, Abram's name would be changed to Abraham and Sarai would become Sarah. They received a new identity as they kept walking. There would be no stopping place along the road that led to the promised land. Charles Wesley described this ongoing journey of faith in one of his best hymns: "Changed from glory into glory, till in heaven we take our place" ("Love Divine, All Loves Excelling," *The United Methodist Hymnal*, #384).

Like Abraham and Sarah, we have been on the road together for thirty-one years now. Along the way, we added two daughters and, most recently, our first son-in-law. When we reflect on the spiritual path our marriage has taken, we are drawn to the words of the Sixteenth Psalm:

> The LORD is my chosen portion and my cup;
>   you hold my lot.
> The boundary lines have fallen for me in pleasant places;
>   I have a goodly heritage. (v. 5)

The lines of our journey have fallen in both pleasant and painful places, and, by God's grace, we have learned some lessons along the way.

We have learned that "Every good and perfect gift comes from God."

Those words come from the writer of the New Testament epistle of James (1:17) who, for all we know, may have picked it up from the psalmist who wrote:

I say to the LORD, "You are my Lord;
 I have no good apart from you." (16:2)

I have only had one wife, but I am on my third wedding ring. The second ring disappeared when I dove into the crystal blue water off the coast of Rio de Janeiro. The first ring, the one she placed on my finger on June 14, 1969, had to be cut off after a water skiing accident, in which I could have lost my finger. Marsha had that ring engraved with James 1:17: "Every good and perfect gift comes from God." I have never quite had the nerve to ask if I was God's good gift to her or she was God's good gift to me. We both agree that we were God's good gift to each other.

The lines of our lives converged at a student leader retreat in the fall of 1966. Marsha had left her "home and kindred" in St. Petersburg, and I had left mine in Western Pennsylvania to go to a small Christian college in Kentucky. She was a junior, the vice president of her class, destined to graduate *cum laude* and to be chosen as "Miss Asburian," the highest honor on the campus. I was a lowly sophomore, and when I met her, I was impressed! I might as well confess that I was doing some social climbing when I finagled a way for us to ride back to campus together. On the way back, I asked her for our first date. By the time that date was over, I knew that it was the best thing I had ever done!

The way Marsha tells her story, she had dated several other guys in her first two years of college, but none of those relationships seemed to go anywhere. During the summer before we met, she made her list and checked it twice. She knew exactly what she wanted in the man she would marry, and she offered that list to God in prayer. Although she has never actually shown me the list, she reports that I came close enough to get her thinking that I might be the gift for which she was waiting. I never wrote out a spousal shopping list; but the more I got to know her, the more convinced I became that this was the woman with whom I could spend the rest of my life.

Whatever we knew or thought we knew back then, we now know that each of us is a healthier, stronger, more complete person because of the gifts we have received from each other. The life we share is such a good gift that both of us have been willing to work very hard to make it the best that it can be. But no matter how hard we have worked, no matter how much of our own energy we have poured into it, we know that this life we share is a gift and that every good and perfect gift comes from God.

We have learned the value of Christian friendships.

We are grateful that we have not traveled the road alone. We can shout with the psalmist,

How excellent are the LORD's faithful people!
My greatest pleasure is to be with them! (16:3 TEV)

From the very beginning of our relationship, we have been blessed with Christian friends who have nurtured, encouraged, corrected, and guided us along the way. During those first years of marriage, we joined a small group with three other couples. The group was intended for Bible study and prayer, but the most important lesson we learned was that we were not really crazy after all! Just about the time we ran into something that we had no idea how to handle, one of the other couples would say, "Oh, we've just been through that. For what it's worth, here's how we dealt with it." We learned that the struggles, tensions, conflicts, and adjustments we were facing were all normal stuff. Through our laughter and tears, we learned from each other how to build a healthy marriage.

We experienced the same kind of nurturing friendship during the years we were raising our daughters. Carrie Lynn was in elementary school and Deborah Jeanne in preschool when we joined a group of parents in the "Systematic Training for Effective Parenting" course. Second only to prayer and the grace of God, it was the best resource we found in the task of parenting. All our kids became group projects. With a common set of values and goals, we did our parenting together. Our children knew it was a waste of time to say, "All the other parents are letting their kids do it" because their parents were in cahoots with one another. That circle of parents laughed together, cried together, listened to one another, and supported one another in trying to become the kind of parents our children needed and deserved.

Now, we are empty nesters, starting to look toward retirement. We are learning a whole new pattern of life and love together, and once again, God has given us a circle of friends in which to grow, to test and, to discover the next stage of our journey together.

We have learned to hold on in the hard places.

Regardless of the circumstances, the psalmist lives with great confidence:

I am always aware of the LORD's presence;
he is near, and nothing can shake me. (16:8 TEV)

The Genesis writer tucks an ominous little detail into the very beginning of Abraham and Sarah's journey: "At that time the Cannanites were in the land" (Genesis 12:6). Throughout the early pages of biblical history, whenever there are Cannanites in the land, you can be sure there will be hard times ahead for the Hebrew people. There is no escaping it; that is just the way things are.

Our experience in our own marriage and our observation of others has convinced us that the critical question is not, Will you go through hard places? Mark it down. You will! There are always Cannanites in the land. The critical question is, How will you go through the hard places? Will you hold on together? Will you have the spiritual resources to make it through when the going gets tough? Hard times and difficult places either pull us together or push us apart. It all depends on how we face them.

Our marriage bears the scars of hard places along the way. We have faced death: the death of my father, the death of friends and relatives, the death of our daughters' teenage peers. We have had times when we disappointed each other, our children disappointed us, and we disappointed them. We have been through times when money was tight, and we had to find a way to make it to the next paycheck. We have gone through times when external circumstances created stress in our relationship. We have faced health crises that forced us to deal with our mortality. We have faced Cannanites in the land.

But in each crisis, we found the grace to use those hard times to pull us together rather than to push us apart. We have learned to hold on in the hard places and to search for God's presence in the middle of our struggles. And we have always found God's grace to see us through. We have discovered that the Lord is always with us. Like the psalmist says, nothing can shake our confidence that in every stage of our journey, God is with us, and to the degree that we allow it, God will turn that painful place into a place of growth, strength, healing, and blessing in our lives.

We have learned that healthy relationships, like healthy bodies, are the result of hard work and discipline.

When the psalmist says, "I have served you faithfully" (16:10, paraphrase), I hear the witness of a person who has invested the hard work and discipline that healthy relationships require. When counseling with engaged couples, I try to tell them something that none of the wedding consultants or florists will tell them. I tell them something they will not hear from the limousine driver on the way from the wedding to the reception. I want them to know that healthy marriages, like healthy bodies, are the result of regular discipline and hard work.

The truth is that we have worked very hard at our marriage. It's been fun. It's been rewarding. But it has also taken hard work and discipline. It takes a great deal of discipline to protect time for each other, particularly when one of us is a recovering workaholic! It took hard work to focus our time and energy on our daughters. It takes discipline to continue to invest in each other and not be drawn toward any other persons to meet our deepest emotional and sexual needs.

In a very practical sense, it has taken sheer discipline and Marsha's tight grip on the checkbook to organize our finances around our commitment to Christ. The cause of gigantic amounts of conflict in marriages today is not just the high cost of living, but the cost of high living. It took discipline to tithe, to give God the first tenth of our income, particularly in those early years when we lived in neighborhoods where everyone else around us had a whole lot more money than we did. It was hard to resist the tempting allure of the credit card demon. It took hard work to order our finances around our commitment to Christ.

It's been hard work, but wonderfully rewarding work. The payoff has been more than worth the investment. There's no doubt in our minds that healthy relationships, like healthy bodies, are the result of hard work and discipline.

We have learned that joy comes in obedience to the will of God.

God's promise to Abram and Sarai was that they would become a great nation and that through them "all the families of the earth shall be blessed" (Genesis 12:3). Their journey began with the promise that obedience to the call of God would result in great joy for them and joyful blessings for the whole creation. The psalmist celebrates that same promise with this affirmation:

You will show me the path that leads to life;
your presence fills me with joy. (16:11 TEV)

We have discovered that God keeps that promise and that the way of obedience is the way of joy.

Our first big decision, a decision that shaped the rest of our life together, was where we would go after I completed seminary. Would we return to Western Pennsylvania where I had grown up and served as a summer intern? Or would we go to Florida, where I would be a stranger and soon discover whether or not the church would take me in? Looking back from this vantage point, it is difficult to imagine why the choice was so hard, but at the time, it was the most difficult decision we had ever faced.

We talked with our family and friends. We counseled with our pastor. We prayed for God's will to be made clear to us. We kept waiting for God to write the directions in the sky. We watched for a sign. But a sign never came. There have, in fact, been very few times in our lives when we have been absolutely sure of God's will before we stepped out on it. Finally, our pastor forced us to a decision. If I intended to apply for admission to the Florida Conference of The United Methodist Church, it was time to begin the process. Based on the little bit we knew, we simply prayed, "Lord, we're not at all sure where you want us to go, but we are going to take the step toward Florida. If this is your will, then please confirm it. If it is not your will, please close the door and lead us another way." We stepped out in that testing faith, and for thirty years God has continued to confirm that decision by continuing to open new doors for us.

Somewhere in the earliest stages of my faith, I learned that the way to joy leads through the pathway of obedience. Someone, somewhere, taught me that when we feel God's call, the only appropriate response is, "Yes." We have discovered that in saying yes to God, we have been led in a path that ultimately leads to joy.

Like Abraham and Sarah's journey, ours has had its full share of twists, turns, and surprising detours. There have been bumps in the road and rough places that needed to be made plain. But we can sing the old gospel song, "I Wouldn't Take Nothin' for My Journey Now." It has become a journey filled with great joy. Because of what we have learned along the way, we intend to keep walking along the path together, "as long as life shall last."

While I was working on the final draft of this chapter, I received a Christmas letter from a couple we had known in a previous congregation. Both of them are over eighty years old now and have their share of physical limitations that come with the aging process. He has a history of heart trouble. For the twenty or so years I have known them, he has always been absolutely honest about the realities of life and death. The letter reported that this Christmas day they celebrated fifty-nine years "of wonderful, loving marriage" and that they are looking ahead to the sixtieth. He reminisced about how their journey began: "Sure glad she came to Orange City, Iowa, to teach Latin where I used to feed her every day at the dear old Corner Café." And he looked to the inevitable future: "When that time comes, Pastor Bill is going to inter us together in St. Luke's Memorial Garden, which I helped start at the behest of Jim Harnish many moons ago. You are all invited to attend." He closed the letter with this affirmation of the joyful mystery of love, marriage, and eternal life: "Think of us together where we believe we can continue to be loving soul mates on the Other Side." That's what it means to be "two for the road" for a long, long time!

7

Communicating in the Family: Things to Avoid Like the Plague

June and James W. Moore

Communication—between individuals and within families—how vital that is! Good communication can bring peace and harmony. Bad communication can trigger discord and suspicion. Good communication can facilitate healing. Bad communication can cause pain and sickness. Good communication can produce and enhance love. Bad communication can spread bitterness and hostility. To think about this, consider two quick stories. Notice the common thread that runs through them.

The first story is about two men who met on the road one day. One said, "Hey, I know you. You're the guy from Maine who made a million dollars in potatoes." The other fellow answered, "Well, you almost got that right. It wasn't Maine; it was Georgia. It wasn't potatoes; it was cotton. It wasn't *made* a million dollars; it was *lost* a million dollars. And it wasn't me; it was my brother. Other than that, you got it just right."

The second story is about a pastor who went back to visit a church he had served many years ago. As he walked into the fellowship hall, he saw Betty. She and her husband, Willy, had been faithful members of the church and dear friends. The pastor was delighted to see Betty. He rushed over, shook her hand, and said, "Betty, I'm so glad to see you. How are you doing? And how is your good husband, Willy?" Betty responded, "Haven't you heard? Willy's gone to heaven." Without thinking, the pastor said, "I'm sorry." Then he thought that was not the right thing to say about somebody who had gone to heaven. So, trying to correct it, he said, "I mean, I'm glad." Well, that was worse. And then he blurted out, "I mean, I'm surprised!" Sometimes the more we say the worse it gets!

The thread that runs through these stories is the problem of communication. Good communication means life and hope and joy. Bad communication means death and despair and defeat. Good communication can inspire our soul and lift our spirit. Bad communication can poison our minds and twist our thinking. Communication is so important!

Remember the old Henny Youngman joke about the man who went to the doctor and said, "Doc, every time I do my hand like this, it hurts." And the doctor responded, "Well, don't do that. Don't do that anymore!"

There are certain actions in the family, in marriage, in our relationships with people, that are so hurtful, so harmful, so destructive, that the only counsel is "Don't do that! Don't do that anymore!" But there are practical effective Christian techniques for communicating. Now, let us suggest some things that we need to beware of and to avoid when we are trying to communicate in the family.

Beware of Mind Games

A mind game is a game we create in our minds to test someone's love for or loyalty to us—when they do not know the game and do not know they are being tested. Mind games are unfair, and we should avoid them like the plague. For example, you might think something like this, "If my daughter really loves me, then she will call me this afternoon at 2:00." But, you see, that is unfair. She does not know that you want or expect that. Or, you might think, "If my son loves me, he will clean up his room before 5:00 P.M." Again, that is unfair. He does not know that is what you want. He does not know he is being tested.

Have you ever been with someone when everything is going along smoothly, and then all of the sudden, the other person starts pouting or becomes angry with you or acts hurt? You feel as if you have walked into the middle of a movie. What happened? Well, what happened was that someone played a mind game on you—and you did not read that person's mind and did not know what was expected. But, you see, that is unfair. How can you rise to the occasion if you do not know what the occasion is?

Let us give a classic illustration of the silliness of mind games. Imagine that a young man and woman are going to have a romantic dinner: candlelight, nice music—just the two of them—and gourmet hamburgers. They sit down at the beautifully appointed table, hold hands, and offer a prayer. The woman is hungry, so she quickly fixes her hamburger and begins eating.

The man sees the ketchup on the other side of the table close to her. So he plays a mind game. He thinks, "She knows I like ketchup on my hamburgers. Why doesn't she pass me the ketchup? Look at her feeding her face while I'm starving. If she loved me, she would pass me the ketchup. If she really loved me, she would be thinking of me. Well, I won't eat! I'm just going to sit here and see how long it takes for her to realize that I need the ketchup."

All of the sudden, she looks up and sees him pouting, moping, seething, and she cannot figure it out. So she says to him, "Honey, is something wrong?" And he screams, "Do you have to ask?" What started out as a nice romantic evening becomes a disaster that easily could have been avoided. How? By his simply saying, "Would you please pass me the ketchup? I love ketchup on my hamburgers!" It is so simple and yet so profound.

Some years ago, June and I were doing a television interview with a psychologist, and we asked him, "What is the number one problem in marriages and families in America today?" Without hesitating, he said, "No question about it. The biggest problem in families today is the crazy notion we have that if we have to ask for something—if we have to tell people what we are thinking, wanting, needing, or expecting—that it's second rate." He said, "Amazingly, we think that if somebody loves us, that person should be able to read our minds." That is silly and unfair. The point is, we have to tell each other what we want, need, feel, think, and expect. But let us hurry to say that we need to tell each other tenderly and lovingly. Beware of mind games. They only lead to heartache, confusion, and sometimes disaster.

Beware of Wrong Pronouns

The wrong pronoun is "you" with a pointed finger. The right pronoun is "I" with open hands. When we say "you" with a pointed finger, communication immediately breaks down. When we say "I" with open hands, people lean forward to listen. The "you" pronoun is especially bad when we add the word "always" or "never." "You always," "You never" do not get a hearing or a response—only a negative reaction.

Let us illustrate what we mean. Suppose that we could put our daughter, Jodi, into a time machine and take her back to the time when she was sixteen years old. Imagine that she wants to go to a party, but the rumor has gotten out that the party may be a bit wild—and she knows that we have heard the rumor. Now, here are two different scenarios.

In the first one, she uses the wrong pronoun ("you" with the pointed finger). She comes in and says, "Mom and Dad, I know how you are. I know what you think, and I know what you are going to say, but I don't care. I'm going to that party, and you can't stop me!" What are we going to do? We are going to think, "This young lady needs to be straightened out!" And we are going to list all of the reasons she should not go to the party.

Here is scenario two, using the right pronoun ("I" with open hands). She comes to us and says, "Mom and Dad, I need to talk with you for a few minutes about something that is really important to me. I want to go to a party on Friday. It's important to me, and let me try to explain why." She gives us her reasons. Then she says, "Now, I know about the rumors. I have heard them, too. But I also know how to act, and I can go to that party and have a good time, and I can do it in a way that will make my family proud of me." Why, we will go fill up the car with gas for her because she used the right pronoun!

It is so simple and yet so profound. Whenever we say "you" with a pointed finger, communication breaks down; and whenever we say "I" with open hands, people lean forward to listen. Try it out, and you will be amazed at what happens.

Beware of Dumping Emotional Garbage on the Dinner Table

There is a time and place to discuss emotional things. Dinner is not one of them. But you know what happens to us: We live at such a hectic, frantic pace that when we get to the dinner table, we think we have a captive audience, so we go for the jugular. There are times when we just need to love and celebrate one another and be thankful to God for one another and for life and love.

In the early days of the church, holy communion was a full meal where the church family came together to celebrate God's love and God's goodness and their love and what they had in common and shared together. The goal was to commune with God and with one another in a sense of peace, joy, gratitude, love, and celebration. In the Christian home, every meal should be that kind of holy communion— a time to celebrate, not a time to attack one another.

A psychologist friend of ours illustrates this graphically. He says, "Imagine that you are having dinner with your family when all of a sudden someone gets up, gets the garbage can, and begins to drop garbage all over the table. That wouldn't be very appetizing, would it?" Yet that is what we do with emotional garbage, isn't it? We need to avoid that like the plague. Let dinnertime, let mealtime in the Christian home be Holy Communion where we celebrate God's love for us and our love for God and for one another.

Beware of What Is Put into Words

When God created the world, God spoke it into existence: "Let there be light and there was light." A lot of things get spoken into existence. If I say, "I don't trust you" enough, the reality is created. We can hurt or punish people with words. We can make people sick or destroy them with words. So we need to be very careful about what we put into words.

The "good news" is that we can help and heal people with words. The words of encouragement, of appreciation, of kindness, of love can work incredible miracles. The point is clear. We only have so much breath, so use it to form words that build up, not words that tear down. Beware of mind games. Beware of wrong pronouns, beware of dumping emotional garbage on the dinner table, and beware of what you put into words.

Beware of Misusing the First Four Minutes

Let us clarify this because it is very important, and we urge you to try it out right away. The "first four minutes" concept is the idea that the most important moments in any encounter are the first four minutes. Let us show you what we mean. In any interpersonal relationship (family, marriage, friendship, work, and so on), two or more people come together. They are united, one, bonded. But then there are times when they go apart. They go to work, to school, to sleep, out of town, and then they come back together.

They re-enter the relationship; and the most significant time is the first four minutes of re-entry. Why? Because deep down inside, all of us have insecure feelings, and we come back to a relationship wondering, "Is it still all right here for me? Am I still loved? Am I still accepted?" As we re-enter the relationship, we subconsciously want and need affirmation. So, the first four minutes should be spent in affirming each other, loving each other, hugging each other, stroking each other, welcoming each other, celebrating each other. If we affirm each other for four minutes, then no one feels personally attacked if later we have to deal with problems.

So, each of us might say, "When I come home at night, love me for four minutes, and then tell me I'm late. Love me for four minutes, and then ask me where I've been. Love me for four minutes, and then tell me the dog broke our favorite lamp. Love me for four minutes, and then tell me that Roger Mudd and the crew from *60 Minutes* are in the den and want to talk to me. Love me for four minutes, and then show me the letter from the Internal Revenue Service."

Now, this is true for every human being. We all need the first four minutes of love and affirmation. Children need it, wives need it, husbands need it, mothers need it, friends need it, coworkers need it, everybody needs it—just four minutes of encouragement and acceptance. It is so important. Try it out, and you will be amazed.

Beware of Neglecting God and God's Church

What does it take to communicate well in the family? Love, respect, thoughtfulness, patience, tenderness, compassion, empathy, gratitude, effort, commitment. We do not know nearly as much as we would like to know about those great qualities, but what little we do know about them, we learned from God at church.

In the prologue to John's Gospel, Jesus is called the Word of God. What does that mean? Simply this: Jesus was God's idea for us, God's plan for us, God's truth for us—wrapped up in a person. God's word became flesh and dwelt among us. Jesus came to show us what God is like and what God wants us to be. So, Jesus is the measuring stick—the pattern, the model, the example, the blueprint—for communicating. And when Jesus spoke, people heard and saw and felt God. That's our calling, isn't it?

Speak that people can hear through our frail words and actions the eternal word of God. Speak that our words fill the air not with the sounds of hate and hostility, not with the sounds of temper or cruelty, not with the sounds of jealousy or vengeance or self-pity, but with the words of life—the words of love!

8

Loving, Honoring, and Cherishing

Bonnie J. and Donald E. Messer

Married in the mid-1960s, we were among the first wave of do-it-yourself liturgists who felt compelled to rewrite the traditional Christian wedding ceremony. In reality, our revisioning proved not very radical, as we stood in the church sanctuary, pledging our love to each other and vowing to care for each other as long as we both would live. (In contrast, our son and daughter-in-law came to their wedding site in canoes and invoked not only contemporary Christian images, but also references from Judaism and other religions!) Family and friends were invited to join in the special prayer we penned:

> Grant unto this young couple the divine grace and guidance necessary for their marriage that they may live in Christian love. Look with favor upon their marriage, O God, that they may love, honor, and cherish each other; caring for one another with faithfulness and patience, and persevering together through all tribulation. May their concern for each other and their compassion for others unite them always. . . .

We did not tape these words on our refrigerator as a constant reminder or even regularly reread it. Discovering it again recently, however, we were surprised to realize how well this prayer reflects some of the core beliefs and values that have served as the foundation of our life together.

Building a successful and lasting relationship is a demanding and complex process. No simple slogans will suffice. Bookstores and libraries abound with helpful (and some not so helpful) treatises, offering various approaches to making life's most intimate journey both enjoyable and enduring. What works for one couple or family may not work for another; people are far too diverse and complex to allow for a cookie-cutter, or prescriptive, approach.

71

Five Values in Our Journey

While no single prayer or set of commandments can cover all situations, we seek to offer some insights into what we consider core building blocks to a marriage, which may have some applicability for others. We have identified five values that can be traced in our marriage and spiritual journey together.

First, there is an affirmation of the centrality of our faith in God's grace and our desire to be part of an active faith community in which we can share our joys and concerns. For us, these were practically "givens" that never required any negotiation or compromise.

The organized church has always played a significant part in our lives. We met during activities of the Methodist Youth Fellowship and later attended denominational colleges. Our honeymoon included lugging a rented trailer across the country to seminary in Boston. The first years of our marriage found Don serving as a pastor for an inner-city African American congregation and then in South Dakota parishes. The remainder of our marital life has been lived in the context of a church college and seminary, so in truth there never has been a time when we have explored religious "options" or seriously considered not being involved in the life of a church community.

We recognize that many couples do not bring common experiences and expressions of faith into their relationship. This certainly does not mean such a relationship is impossible, but it does present a special challenge for them to find a meaningful philosophy of life and marriage to undergird their journey together.

Sometimes marriages become unraveled when one partner suddenly discovers Jesus or drifts away from the church. Illustrative of the former was the divorce of Jane Fonda from CNN founder Ted Turner. He claimed her sudden conversion to Christianity was a shock to him. In an interesting case study of marital miscommunication and spiritual integrity, Fonda told the *New Yorker* that "my becoming a Christian upset him very much—for good reason. He's my husband and I chose not to discuss it with him—because he would have talked me out of it. He's a debating champion" (Cited by the Associated Press, "Fonda Files for Divorce from Turner," April 21, 2001). It is questionable how often religious reasons divide a couple or whether they are just symptomatic of communication or other marital problems. However, marital difficulties clearly can be exacerbated when people do not share common faith convictions.

Theologically, we both have embraced a God of loving acceptance and forgiveness. For us, being Christian has been to live our lives with a sense of freedom and personal fulfillment, not to be restricted by narrow religious rules or stultifying scriptural commands. We affirm a God who blesses human intimacy and sexuality as good. We have found joy and happiness in our marriage and family because we believe God cares for us and that through these relationships, we demonstrate care for each other. Marriage and the family have been for us channels by which we continually experience God's love in a human, intimate form. In our loving embraces, in the births and lives of our children and grandchildren, and in our expanding extended family, we miraculously feel a sacred connectedness that links both the human and the divine.

The second value explicit in the wedding prayer was that of loving and honoring each other. Both "love" and "honor" are action verbs, requiring much more than lip service. How frequently one hears persons yearning to feel special, to be "held dear," to be "treated with tenderness." All too frequently, it is easier to lift up a litany of disappointments to one's mate, rather than to affirm how unique and precious he or she is.

Most of us are painfully aware of our shortcomings. We are not eager that our partner become a self-appointed critic or conscience for us. Over the years, some of our greatest interpersonal conflicts have come when we have felt the other was more intent on criticizing than loving us. What a blessing to experience a taste of unconditional love that affirms us, encompassing our faults and failures as well as our talents.

Honoring is an old-fashioned term suggesting respect and prompting expressions of recognition. It may mean telling your partner "thank you" for the little things that one takes for granted—like preparing meals, cleaning the house, or taking out the garbage. Or it can mean expressing pride in your partner's accomplishments at work or in the community. It includes taking seriously each other's viewpoints and avoiding belittling comments that devalue the other. To honor a loved one is to acknowledge how truly special he or she is and how fortunate you feel to be in his or her presence.

Possibly every couple periodically wonders whether they are, in the words of Scott Stanley, creatively "sticking together" or "just stuck" in their marriages (Scott Stanley, *The Heart of Commitment* [Nashville: Thomas Nelson Publishers, 1998], 3). Patterns of communication and lifestyle get set. Usually this feels comfortable and good, but at other times one might feel that the marital journey has got caught in a rut or lost in a detour. Reminding each other of deeper values like loving and honoring may stimulate a stalled love life or jump-start a boring relationship.

Long-lasting marital relationships require discovering and living with the noble arts of compromise and forgiveness. When persons have different interests, hopes, and aspirations, finding sufficient commonalities and commitments becomes a continuing challenge. A Jewish Yom Kippur prayer underscores the need for forgiveness and starting over:

> The leaves are beginning to turn from green to red and orange. The birds are beginning to turn and heading once more toward the South. The animals are beginning to turn to storing their food for the winter. For leaves, birds, and animals, turning comes instinctively. But for us turning does not come so easily. It takes an act of will for us to make a turn. It means breaking with old habits. It means admitting that we have been wrong and this is never easy. It means losing face; it means starting all over again; and this is always painful. It means saying: I am sorry. It means recognizing that we have the ability to change. These things are terribly hard to do. But unless we turn, we will be trapped forever in yesterday's ways. (Chaim Stern, ed. *Gates of Repentance: The New Union Prayerbook for the Days of Awe* [New York: Central Conference of American Rabbis, 1978], 372)

While this Yom Kippur prayer was not specifically written about marriages, it reminds us that successful relationships require couples who are committed to change, willing to admit mistakes, free to forgive each other, and are daily willing to start once again. It calls us to break from "yesterday's ways" and discover anew love and life in each other.

The third value is closely related to the second: "Cherishing" each other has been indispensable for our marital and family journey. To "cherish" is to treasure your partner and the gift of human love one has been given. Too often relationships rupture because we forget what a privilege and joy it is to know and be with each other. Or we neglect to polish that treasure by spending sufficient time and energy to create feelings of worth and meaning.

Our daughter and son-in-law recently complimented us when they asked for a poster that we had framed years ago and hung in our bedroom. They wanted to display it in their new home. The photo would not win any artistic awards, but it showed a young father walking down a wooded lane carrying his toddler daughter. The caption underneath reads: "Take the Time."

74

Slogans, of course, have their limitations, and none can ever quite comprehend the complexity of enjoyable marital and family life. But "take the time" effectively served as a reminder for us over the years of the importance of spending not only quality, but also quantity time with each other and with our children. All the best theories in the world combined with all the best intentions amount to naught, if there is no time or space set aside to practice them. With the ever-escalating pace of marital and family life, setting aside sufficient hours and days for each other becomes critically important. Occasions for shared times have always been given high priority. Whether it was vacations in the United States or travels abroad, the chance to affirm our love and caring for each other while learning about other cultures has provided a rich opportunity for growth in our relationships.

Years ago, a popular maxim claimed that "the family that prays together, stays together." Though we raised our children in a church context, we have never been particularly public in our prayers, except for faithfully offering grace at our meals (often by singing the Johnny Appleseed song: "Oh, the Lord's been good to me").

Perhaps our spiritual aphorism was more secularized: "The family that plays together, stays together." Because not all of us are athletic, we have not been big outdoor campers or engaged in rough-and-tumble sport activities. Rather, we have translated our "playing together" into playing board games, being athletic spectators, swimming, vacationing, and less strenuous activities like miniature golf. Even now as we have become "empty nesters," we usually set aside time every evening to play a game that challenges and nourishes our competitive and playful spirits. We are convinced marriages and families survive and thrive if they have consistent "fun times" together.

Fourth, both of us entered marriage with a commitment to protecting and nurturing our relationship and the family we hoped to create. Throughout our marriage, there has been a strong sense of commitment. We were in this relationship for the long run. Divorce was understandable and acceptable for others, but not for us. As our son once wrote us: "Love has no expiration date."

Certainly, some days and months were easier and more enjoyable than others, but there was never the fear that our partner would suddenly walk out. There was never the worry that "if I screw up one more time, my partner will just throw in the towel." Central to Bonnie's approach to counseling and in our marriage has been a contemporary definition of agape love: "In my presence, you are safe." We were well aware that we were not perfect partners, but we were also aware of a sense of permanence, which affirmed our individuality and allowed for freedom to stretch and grow. Through our struggles to love and understand and forgive each other, we experienced with new appreciation the meaning of God's love and grace.

The writer of Ecclesiastes 4:11 asked: "How can one be warm alone?" (RSV). We have recognized the importance of shared experiences and have struggled to find adequate time to be together. It is difficult to love and care for someone in absentia. Our belief in the necessity of continually nurturing our relationship has resulted in a concerted effort to regularly communicate with each other. While our communication may not be perfect, it has been frequent! Even when work has required that we be apart, we look forward to nightly long-distance calls to keep in touch. As much as has been humanly possible with our demanding schedules, we have tried to preserve Friday evening as "date night." (Bonnie's number one pet peeve is airlines' policy of providing cheaper fares if one stays over Saturday night. She labeled it an "antifamily" and an "anti-healthy-marriage" policy.)

Stephen R. Covey, in *First Things First: To Live, to Love, to Learn, to Leave a Legacy* (New York: Simon & Schuster, 1995) emphasizes establishing priorities in life by illustrating that a jar can hold a number of large rocks, if they are put inside first (cited in Scott Stanley, *The Heart of Commitment: Cultivating Lifelong Devotion in Marriage* [Nashville: Thomas Nelson, 1998], 36-37). However, if pebbles, sand, and water are inserted first, then fewer rocks can be included. Similarly, we need to look at what we put into our "marriage jar" first. What are our priorities? For us, this has meant spending a lot of time and energy working on coordinating our schedules. Don's work as a college and seminary president for thirty years has required much traveling. This was carefully balanced with time for the family and for our relationship. Prioritizing proved essential. Not every meeting could be on the top of the to-do list. Our children's activities, and now the activities of our grandchildren, as well as Bonnie's work as a psychologist, all require attention.

It is easy to fill our jar with the pebbles and sand of multiple committee meetings, personal interests, and other "shoulds," leaving little space for the more significant persons and activities that nurture our soul and our relationships. The demands of this hi-tech age seem to require instant responses to E-mails, rather than to the needs of our partners. It is a constant challenge to keep our priorities in mind. Many times the prioritizing becomes very difficult when there are several strong compelling needs. For example, when Don was invited to speak at an AIDS conference in India over Thanksgiving weekend, we struggled to find a way to honor Don's desire to attend the conference and yet honor our need to be together at special holiday family times.

A fifth dimension of our wedding prayer accented a strong affirmation of our "compassion for others." Balancing these commitments has been both a guiding force and the source of many struggles in our marriage. Sometimes, but not always, compassion for others becomes the deciding factor in making decisions. In the instance mentioned above, we decided Don should make the conference a priority because of our joint desire to combat this global disease and the discrimination so often associated with it.

Relationships can be enhanced when couples embrace a shared social commitment or concern for others. Both of us affirm the importance of actively working to improve the world in which we live. While we both feel responsible to help make the world a better place, our areas of expertise and perceived responsibility have diverged. Sometimes this results in serious conflicts.

Don has loved the life of secular and church politics, while Bonnie has found little meaning or satisfaction in either. Bonnie has sought to minister to persons individually or as couples in her private practice as a psychologist, while Don has always seen "the world as his parish" and continually seeks new opportunities to be in mission in a global context. A special pleasure for us is when we can combine our areas of concern and expertise, such as recently when we were both able to go to India and lead HIV/AIDS workshops.

Related to compassion for others has been our shared belief in the importance of affirming differences and celebrating diversity. Intolerance of differences and diversity can endanger relationships, while embracing and affirming differences and diversity enriches the spiritual journey of life.

Over the years, our family encountered new and different cultural customs and practices. While not always comfortable with them, we have learned to affirm them as "different" rather than as "wrong" or even as unusual. Likewise in our marriage, we frequently have been painfully aware of how different we are from each other. Bonnie can be quite content with a quiet evening at home, while Don is happier when constantly active. Bonnie loves gardening, while Don finds no pleasure in yard work. Don enjoys the pace of modern urban life, while Bonnie yearns for smaller, less crowded cities. We could go on and on! But after thirty-seven years of married life, we confess that we have not been able to change each other's ways or preferences, and see no hope for significant transformations in the future!

At the heart of our relationship has been an appreciation for God's great gift of diversity. Over the years, our lives and our children's have been greatly enriched by our friendship with persons of other colors, cultures, nationalities, religions, and sexual orientations. Our sense of family is not exclusive to one tribe, but inclusive and ecumenical, celebrating the whole human community.

In Conclusion

Over the years, we have talked and toiled along life's journey, sometimes walking literally hand in hand. Occasionally we have wandered adventurously, if not perilously, off on our own paths. Other times we have tried to give our partner an extra tug, hoping the other would see the wisdom of walking down the trail we had individually chosen. Throughout, our common values have helped sustain us and bring us back to a shared quest.

We believe life is a choice of values. In this chapter, we have sought to share some values that have helped guide our journey. The backbone of our marriage has been faith in God's grace and participation in a community of believers; a desire to love, honor, and cherish each other; a lifetime commitment to marriage; and a compassion for others. We do not present our choices as prescriptive for others. Instead we share what has been normative for us, inviting others to rethink what sustains and strengthens them in the exciting spiritual journey of life called marriage.

9

Lucky Thirteen: Ritual, Faith, Marriage

Ulrike and Clifton F. Guthrie

Today is our thirteenth anniversary. It is either an especially auspicious or an especially ominous year for us because we were first married on a Friday the thirteenth. It is our "first" marriage because we were actually married twice. This is "thirteen A," as Uli likes to say. "Thirteen B" comes three weeks later, on June 5.

We had planned to go to a justice of the peace to make our vows in secret. Unlike some "quiet" weddings, ours would be neither a romantic elopement nor an attempt to legitimate an unexpected pregnancy. In fact, we had not yet become husband and wife in the biblical sense. We had been deeply influenced by evangelical traditions that taught us that premarital sex was forbidden and impure. We would gradually grow out of our fixation on sex as the chief measure of holiness. But even at that age, our adherence to the rules was spotty at best: Like so many other Christian couples struggling with their sexuality, we had discovered just how far we could explore the limits of the law when the spirit of it is abandoned.

So it was a matter of neither romance nor lust that we planned to keep our marriage a secret. The reason was more tellingly wrapped up in our sincere and convoluted efforts to please our parents and follow the rules. Cliff was a citizen of the United States, but Uli, though born in Germany, was (and is still) a citizen of the United Kingdom. With some reluctance and rather late in the game, Uli's tradition-minded family was planning an English wedding for us in the local village church. That was on the calendar for June 5, and plans were well under way. Afterward, we would honeymoon in Scotland and then return to Atlanta so Cliff could take up a small pastorate and continue his Ph.D. studies, and Uli continue her work as an editor.

Uli's fiancée visa had been hard enough to arrange, but now the U.S.

Immigration and Naturalization Service warned us that if we flew to England to be married, it could easily take another six months before she would be able to get another visa to return to the United States. Ironically, the only solution was to be married before we flew to England to get married. If we left the country as a married couple, we could enter it again two weeks later without any hassle. (This is one of the lesser-known privileges for heterosexual married couples in America.)

So that's how we came to hatch the plan to be quietly wed by a justice of the peace. We would be married legally, but we would not tell our families or friends so not to detract from the June 5 ceremony.

But as the circled day on the calendar grew closer, we began to reconsider. It may not be clear why until we say something about how we met.

We met on orientation day, before classes had even begun at seminary. Uli, having completed a master's degree in German, had come to Emory University on a scholarship program from St. Andrews University in Scotland and had decided to spend that year abroad at Emory, studying at the university's seminary. Cliff had gone to Emory to prepare for ordination as a United Methodist minister. We were placed in the same small reflection group and had almost all of our classes together. We got to know each other through the weeks as we talked about theology during marathon phone calls and worried about the orthodoxy of our teachers.

Our first "date" was a pastoral visit made to Jesse Pittman, a member of Cliff's church. He would die of emphysema in the veterans' hospital a few months later, but he managed to embarrass us by telling us we made a cute couple, although we had not yet so much as held hands. The first time the "m" word came up was barely a week later. Uli had come to visit the church where Cliff was a youth minister, and a woman offered to make her wedding dress. We complained to each other about pushy parishioners, and we resisted the pressure from a church that valued married men as ministers above all others. Even so, we were attracted to each other and did not mind the pressure that much. We wooed each other, talking about Barth and Tillich, and took the youth group on a mission trip to fix up old homes in Appalachia. We were young, pious, and in love.

We were also poor. After a year at Emory, Uli returned to England to become religious studies editor for Cambridge University Press, where she was paid a pittance and shared a cold, narrow house and a solitary coal fireplace with two friends. Back in Atlanta, Cliff worked on his Ph.D., using a maxed-out gasoline credit card to buy food at the local convenience store, and lived in the basement of a yuppie Dunwoody couple. In exchange for rent, he was the stable boy for three skittish thoroughbreds and a stupid pony and was obliged to praise the accomplishments and extravagant birthday parties of their spoiled three year old. We spent two very difficult years in an international courtship. Uli's family opposed our relationship because they could not see the sense of having paid for her private schooling and educated her for English society only for her to marry an American vegetarian who was an aspiring theologian and Methodist preacher. Still we hung on, despaired, vacillated. We spent our meager resources on international phone calls, letters, and plane tickets and tried to figure out our future.

It all suddenly fell into place, and in such a definitive way, it was surely providence at work. A new editorial position opened in Atlanta for Uli. A new church job opened up for Cliff, just ten miles away. The part-time pastorate came with hardly any salary, but it had a small house with plenty of land to garden and a quiet place to study. We could finally get married.

As we neared the date we set aside for the justice of the peace, it became harder and harder for us to think that we would be married but not act married for those three weeks between May 13 and June 5. Clearly our overripe hormones were talking at us, too, but at a deeper level we sensed that mere adherence to the forms of tradition was not enough to bind us for a life together. We simply could not see ourselves standing before a local judge, getting married, and going our separate ways in the evening. Our life together would be a complex blending of cultures. Uli would be leaving her country for uncouth America (the Deep South, no less), risking her happiness on a graduate student burdened with college loans and whose best hope for a salary would be the mediocre pay of a church or seminary. We felt in our bones that pleasing the family and following the rules was, for us at least, no agenda for a lasting marriage. The rituals that made us wife and husband would have to speak to the losses, complexity, and risk of our marriage. We knew that the English wedding to come, while meaningful and beautiful, would not likely touch the core of our fears, sorrows, joys, and hopes. So we began to plan for an American wedding as well.

Now we had a wedding to plan and no money to spend. We arranged to have the ceremony at the seminary's chapel, which would be free to us. We typed up and photocopied simple invitations and bulletins.

81

Cliff wore his one suit, and Uli her best dress. A friend would bring a camera and act as the official photographer. Those who wanted to join us at a restaurant for a celebratory meal would have to pay their own way—a memory that still embarrasses us. An hour before the ceremony, we made a curious woman at the farmer's market laugh when we told her we were buying flowers, bread, and wine for our wedding that day. But it was a wonderful day. Twenty close friends gathered to witness and bless our marriage. Three dear teachers led the service: Helen Pearson led the singing, Roberta Bondi preached, and Don Saliers proclaimed the Great Thanksgiving and doodled Buxtehude on the organ. But the highlight of the service was our enacted reading of a liturgy we had put together from the Song of Songs, the Bible's best expression of erotic love. "On my bed night after night I sought him whom my soul loves," and "Your breasts are like two fawns, twins of a gazelle," we told each other breathlessly, while the congregation clucked approvingly. And when we joined our hands to say at the end, "Many waters cannot quench love, neither can floods drown it," we thought of the cold Atlantic Ocean and how it had kept us apart for two years—but no more.

Like many young couples, we were initially attracted to the idea of composing our own vows, convinced that only original and contemporary words could do justice to what we felt inside. So we began to write our own vows, only to find how hard it was to do well. Roberta reminded us that the traditional vows were not only beautiful, but also profoundly challenging, and advised us to follow the wisdom of generations of Christians who had used them. So we promised to have, hold, and love each other for better, worse, richer, poorer, in sickness and in health. Thirteen years later, these words still challenge us in ways far beyond anything we were likely to have written for ourselves. We passed the peace and passed the bread. We drank from the cup, asking that the story of our relationship be folded into the larger story of God's work. And after the benediction, we consumed the leftovers and laughed with our friends, silly with happiness.

We were clever enough to allow just enough time between the ceremony and the evening's reception to rush off to the hotel for our first romp together. After escaping from the photographer, we rushed to our old Subaru to discover that it had been ritually decorated with shaving cream and streamers. Our friends had also followed a tradition of putting rocks in the hubcaps (apparently to make noise as they went around). Unfortunately, they knew more about traditions than they did about cars: Our car did not have hubcaps, so the rocks became thoroughly wedged in the brakes. Our photos of that day include several of Cliff looking supremely annoyed while taking off all the tires and cleaning out the stones, Uli looking on dejectedly as the time allotted for our first cavorting slipped away. Somehow, having to wait a few more hours seemed ritually appropriate for us.

But we had our revenge. We had arranged our reception at a fondue restaurant and goaded our friends to gorge themselves on the beer-based cheese dip, knowing from a previous visit the terrible flatulence it produced. Later, we laughed in bed together. Then we tired each other out and went happily to sleep. When the phone rang after midnight, we woke up startled, thinking, "Oh no, they caught us!" But it was only the desk clerk telling us that our car window had been smashed and radar detector stolen. Believe me, we did not care too much.

So this was our first wedding—the American one. It has been said that the purpose of arranging weddings is to give the couple a first major task to complete, to train them to negotiate life together. If so, our first wedding taught us the importance of improvisation and laughter and the likelihood of chaos. In a world of bridal magazines and $50,000 weddings, we discovered that marriage rituals actually work better when they are assembled out of simple elements that carry depth of meaning rather than out of rented candelabras and horse-drawn carriages.

We lived as married people for three weeks before returning to England. Our families knew that immigration rules had required that we be officially married and that the Anglican service would technically be a "blessing" rather than a wedding, but we told them nothing of the first service and slept in separate rooms until the honeymoon, not wanting to dishonor their generosity. Cliff's mom, dad, and older sister flew over from America, as did an old friend who acted as best man. Cliff's younger sister flew in from Lesotho, Africa, where she was stationed in the Peace Corps. Together with a few other friends from his days as a college exchange student to Canterbury, these were the members of the small group that sat on the groom's side of the church. Uli's side was full of relatives from all over Europe and friends from school and college days.

The caricatured British insistence on decorum and proper manners is perhaps more to be found within an upper-middle-class family like Uli's, than in families whose wealth or status allows them genuine social freedom and individual eccentricities. Or at least that is one way to make sense of how her parents chose to plan and conduct the wedding rituals. The service and reception were thoroughly nice and thoughtfully prepared, but at every turn they worried most about making the event socially acceptable. They did not consult us much in the preparation, and where our input was allowed, we seemed always to meet disapproval or an obstacle.

Several examples come to mind. Uli had had a stunning wedding dress made from raw silk—the most delicate shade of rose. Ironically given our pre-marital restraint, her family frowned upon its implied nonvirginal color, and, to her great disappointment, Uli's family never mustered the ability to say how beautiful she looked in it. As a couple, we were committed to inclusive language in our ceremony and the equity between us it implied. We asked only that the words, "let no man put asunder" be read as "let no one put asunder," but the conservative Anglican priest balked at changing a single word of the *Book of Common Prayer*. We both were vegetarians, but the sit-down reception served local lamb. We vaguely remember eating grapefruit that day. Friends and family had come from around the world to honor the day, and there was no time allowed to greet them.

We had agreed with Uli's professor father that in lieu of formal speeches at the reception, we would offer informal toasts. Given parental apprehensions about the match, we tended to agree with his position that the less said the better. But on the morning of the wedding, we became aware of him rushing around the house with a handful of index cards and a pile of books. With a rap on the wine glass to quiet the crowds, he rose at the reception, pulled an inch-thick stack of cards from his jacket, and held forth concerning the ancient Scottish roots of the Guthrie family, the Anglican roots of Methodism, the importance of marriage, and so on. To be honest, he did a commendable job painting a rosy public picture of a marriage that was clearly a personal tragedy for him. Twenty minutes later, the professor sat down and nodded that it was the groom's turn now. Knowing he had been set up to fail, Cliff could only observe that Wesley himself had lived in Georgia, to where he was about to abscond with the good professor's eldest daughter, thank the family and all who had come, and imply how grateful he was to be married to such a wonderful woman so high above his station. The dinner and the speeches left no time for two of Uli's closest friends to play the chamber music they had rehearsed as their wedding gift before they had to leave for the train station. It was about that time that Cliff's klutzy sister fell off her chair at the high table.

It is a bit of a cliché, but in fact we do look back on most of this and laugh now, knowing full well how much tension with the parents was our own fault. We were too quick to take offense and too quick to cause it; we played out our part in the theatrics and misunderstandings.

What we remember most fondly about the English wedding is exactly what we remember so well about the American one: the presence of family and friends from far and near, the beauty of the day, and the ways that people honored the event with their love and attention. Where were there hints of grace? In a brother's girlfriend's help getting the bridesmaid ready. In the thick taste of the fruit wedding cake with slabs of marzipan icing traditional in England. In the gorgeous swag of evergreens over the church entrance, made carefully by Uli's mother, following a German custom. In the tiny bouquets of wildflowers gracing the dinner tables, picked that morning by her family from the woods where she used to play. In the gifts of organ music and scripture reading performed during the service by long-missed friends. In the wonderful Black Forest clock Uli's parents gave us as a wedding gift—always the first thing we unpack and hang when we move houses, and whose sound fills the empty rooms and makes it home. In the hot water bottle and metal teapot tied to the car's bumper by Tim, the youngest of her three brothers, clanging as we drove north to Scotland (Uli is well known to be inordinately fond of cozy beds and hot tea). These are the ritual elements that continue to hold meaning for us after thirteen years.

The ritual studies scholar Ronald Grimes has lamented that in our culture we have lost the ability to perform rituals that really work. Our weddings do not wed. We spend enormous amounts of money putting together the elements of our wedding ritual in the hope that spending enough will make the ritual more likely to "take" and our marriages last for the lifetimes we promise each other. Grimes's point is that at least some of the blame for our high divorce rate has to do with the insipid and overly sentimental wedding ceremonies we conduct. Our marriages do not last because they avoid truth at the start.

When Cliff was a pastor, we noticed how many American wedding rituals were actually controlled by the photographer. Each ritual moment was set up primarily for the photographic opportunity it presented: drinking champagne with arms intertwined, feeding each other cake, throwing birdseed, throwing the bouquet. Each part of the day is carefully choreographed by a photographer—whose tastes are clearly too influenced by blurry pictures on greeting cards—before the couple is ushered on to the next ritual station.

But somehow our weddings wed. The strange combination of the hasty American ceremony and the more formal English one encompassed and reflected the stories we brought to our marriage and wove them into one. We have no videotapes of those days and cannot imagine their usefulness if we did. The memories we have are far richer, and more binding, than any captured image. Like good jazz, ritual form and improvisation combined to create something new that is fragile yet firm—our marriage. We are at the stage of our lives where the first, and now too often the second, marriages of our friends are failing. Every time we hear of a new separation or divorce between our friends, it sends us into an episode of despair and anxiety, especially for their children, but also for ourselves. Of the marriages of our closest friends, ours is one of the few survivors. We are grateful. We are also deeply aware of the many ways we fail our marriage and the times when its survival has seemed uncertain. Roberta Bondi said in her sermon to us on May 13 that one of our most important tasks in marriage is to nurture our delight in each other: "You did not summon it or choose it; it is a gift given to you by God. Remember that human delight, unlike God's, is very fragile. Being inconsiderate in little ways on an everyday basis will kill it."

Now that we have two children, Thomas and Emelia, this ritual weaving of our stories into our life together seems to be more important than ever. From Uli's family on the other side of the world, we deliberately incorporate family traditions from Uli's English and German traditions into our American lives, such as daily afternoon teatime, to keep that heritage strong and give our lives a ritual backbone. We find ourselves keeping the rhythm of the church year, as taught by Uli's mother, painting hollow Easter eggs to adorn first bare, then budding, then resplendently green birch twigs every Lent; we celebrate St. Nicholas Day on December 6, leaving children's shoes outside the door so that the good Saint can leave in them small presents. We spend Sunday evenings in Advent practicing songs and carols around the candlelit wreath, albeit in English only, not German also; and we decorate our Christmas tree with red apples, straw stars, and white candles (instead of electric lights). These mix nicely with tree ornaments that continue a tradition from Cliff's family: Each child buys one new ornament every year, so that when they establish their own homes, they have the beginnings of their own tree decorations. So when Tom or Emelia hang their new ornament next to a straw star or a grubby green reindeer marked "Cliff 1972" on the bottom, they sense that tradition binds them to their roots.

A patchwork quilt that Uli started sewing at age eight (and remained in progress until after Tom was born) has become a particularly loved symbol of this treasure of heritage passed on from one generation and country to another. It is made from small squares of fabric left over from clothes Uli's mother made for herself and her five children. On nights when Tom is anxious, or just wants to delay bedtime, he asks Uli to tell a story of a patch from the quilt. And so she tells him the story of his grandmother's maternity dress or of a favorite pair of pajamas made of blue checkerboard cloth and small red bears holding balloons. So patch by patch, Tom learns the stories of Uli's family, the stories of hard work and hard times, the stories of care and creativity and concern and exuberant color. The stories cover him in the darkness.

Later, for Emelia, Uli patched another quilt, which was finished much faster! Toward the end of the piecing, Cliff's mother invited her to bring down from the guestroom two brown suitcases that had long sat under the bedside table. They were full of fabric samples that had belonged to Cliff's paternal grandmother, "Guffy"—the grandchildren's burbled contraction of "grandma Guthrie." These are the cases that Guffy had schlepped around to dry goods stores in Appalachian Kentucky during the depression as a traveling saleswoman who suddenly had to support the family when her husband died. What an honor to be allowed to choose samples to include in the patchwork for Emelia, adding another rich story of another mother who provided for her family! And now, four years after this patching together of two families' lives and stories into one, Tom has started his own patchwork quilt, combining some patches left over from that first quilt Uli started at his age, with the ones from Guffy's sample cases, and leftovers from the first quilt, and new bought fabrics that simply catch his eye and imagination. Whose small body will that quilt cover some day? What stories will be told?

Grimes has written that good rituals are both organic and negotiated. That is, they grow naturally out of our lives, but they need to be cultivated and cared for. But as we have found when we fight over where we should hang stockings at Christmas (the mantel or the bedpost), effective rituals are also negotiated: "Ritual is not only something we grow but also something we fight over, fight with, and fight for" (Ronald L. Grimes, *Marrying and Burying: Rites of Passage in a Man's Life* [Boulder, Colo.: Westview Press, 1995], 5).

In the wedding vows we said thirteen years ago, we discovered that the ritual words grown from the wisdom of earlier Christians both supported and challenged. Yet we also fought for changes. In the same way, the traditions we have grown up in and fought over as a couple have been of enormous value in patching our lives together. Like many modern nuclear families, we do not live close to our extended families, and we have moved too often—seven new communities in thirteen years. But we never have to reinvent our lives from scratch or make it up as we go along. We carry these rituals with us wherever we go, and like the Black Forest clock, hear them sound through our lives. It may be more truthful to say that the traditions carry us.

And then there are the rituals, like our Atlanta wedding, that arise more spontaneously and are ours alone. On Tom and Emelia's birthdays, they pile into bed with us as soon as they waken and beg us to tell again the story of their births. We cover them with the stories of how we rushed to the hospital, lost the car keys, and ate potato chips with friends in the recovery room—and they know they are children who are yearned for and are delighted in. And we remember what Roberta told us thirteen years ago today, that human delight, unlike God's, is very fragile.

10

Words Matter: Marriage and the Language of Faith

Esther Kwon Arinaga with Clifford Iwao Arinaga

While driving along a major boulevard in downtown Honolulu a few months ago, we noticed the car in front slowing down at the intersection ahead. Every window of what was once a stylish hatchback was covered with reddish-brown dust. Pockets of rust dotted the rear fenders. But what arrested our attention, as our car pulled up behind, was a torn, faded bumper sticker framed in red, white, and blue, its message still readable—"*Don't mess with marriage.*" Ideas about marriage and the spiritual journey had been on our minds, so we looked at each other and almost in unison cried out, "What's that supposed to mean?"

Words and their meanings have held a fascination for Clifford and me ever since we first met on the steps of the University of Hawaii library in the late 1940s. Bumper stickers, especially, entertain or invite discussion as we pass the time at a traffic stop. As we waited for the light to change that morning, we pondered the author's intent in writing this provocative directive. With debates on the definition of marriage filling the air waves and the halls of our state legislature, we first thought this might be a clarion call from those who oppose marriage between partners of the same sex: *Don't tamper with the definition of traditional marriage.* But the bumper sticker looked too frayed and weathered and the car too dated for that relatively recent issue in our community. We then thought the words might be a throwback to the 1960s when young people everywhere seemed to say, *Don't bother to get married.* As the light turned green, we arrived at a third possibility, the one that we felt was the most meaningful: *Marriage is sacred; don't destroy its sanctity.*

We believe that most couples begin life together with the earnest hope and faith that marriage is a sacred institution. Even if they lack a religious background, they choose to marry in a church or temple and to recite their mutual promises in the presence of a clergyperson and witnesses. In Hawaii where nature provides many awe-inspiring settings, couples often stand before an outdoor altar—by a waterfall or at the edge of the ocean—and experience God's presence in the sound of cascading water or rolling surf.

Biblical verses read during a wedding also affirm the sanctity of marriage. In a familiar passage often heard, the apostle Paul laid out a spiritual road map for couples starting on their marital journey:

> Love is patient and kind; love is not jealous or boastful; it is not arro-
> gant or rude. Love does not insist on its own way; it is not irritable or
> resentful; it does not rejoice at wrong but rejoices in the right. Love
> bears all things, believes all things, hopes all things, endures all things.
> (1 Corinthians 13:4-7 RSV)

Those words resonated throughout the stone chapel during our wedding. Like many newlyweds, we probably thought of love as an abstraction, its meaning diffused, as if seen through a prism. Love was a jewel or a measure of perfection, a sign of joy or a sentiment. Sometimes love was a question mark or a challenge raised during a marital dispute: "Don't you love me?" As a spiritual concept, love was simply an ideal.

Most of us laughingly confess that soon after the wedding ceremonies, the hearts and flowers of romance began to fade and disappear in rapid fashion, a signal that the honeymoon is over. As we look back on our marriage of nearly five decades, we realize that our *spiritual* honeymoon was also brief. As Christians, we had easily embraced the sacred and holy symbols but had little understanding of their importance as a wellspring of faith in marriage. Youth and inexperience clouded our vision. Questions about the spiritual meaning of life and marriage had not yet taken hold. We had no idea that as newlyweds, we were about to embark as soul mates on a spiritual journey—one that would test our faith and ultimately deepen our understanding of spirituality in marriage.

Why did we appear so fickle about the spiritual touchstones of marriage soon after our wedding? The reasons are undoubtedly many and varied, but one explanation frequently mentioned today by writers describing their own spiritual journeys is instructive: It is our penchant to keep matters of individual faith hidden from each other and from the outside world. We are fearful of intolerance, of exposing weaknesses in our marriage, and worse, of being lumped together with "some flaky and reactionary people who use the language of spirituality" (Michael Lerner, *Spirit Matters,* Hampton Roads, 2000). A recent essay by Roger Rosenblatt—author, public-television commentator, and journalist—further confirms this pervasive fear in our country. He reported that Americans like to consider themselves a "religious" people but become uneasy when faith issues like praying, reading the Bible, and becoming "born again" are discussed. Rosenblatt found it curious that we can proclaim "In God We Trust" on our legal tender yet find it threatening to talk about our own spiritual beliefs. Perhaps this is the same reason many couples feel discomfort talking or even thinking about their spiritual needs and yearnings. Even spiritual joys and mystical encounters go unmentioned in marriage. We keep our lives of faith hidden, out of public view and earshot.

Our silence about the spiritual journey in marriage became visually evident at a recent gathering honoring friends' fiftieth wedding anniversary. As part of the evening's program, their son had assembled a slide show of photographs spanning five decades. We caught glimpses of the couple on their wedding day, their faces radiant and expectant. Snapshots in black and white and color followed in quick succession. There were pictures of many "firsts"—their first car, house, child, and place of employment. The photo journal moved seamlessly to scenes of Malaysia, Indonesia, and The Netherlands—places where the couple had lived and worked. Overall, the slide show was a triumphant look at a long and successful marriage. But a few days later, as we talked with our friends about the pictures and the things we had learned about them, we all realized that something important was missing from their lovely marital portrait. It all looked too easy. Where were the moments of crisis, the doubts and misgivings they had felt about each other and about marriage, the expectations that had gone unfulfilled, the sorrows and occasionally overwhelming disappointments endured? More important, where were the scenes of their journey of faith, the snapshots of the spiritual values that had sustained them for fifty years? Our friends quietly agreed that their marital journey was often made easier—more bearable—by their strong faith.

The darker scenes of marriage are never easy to describe. They are probably inappropriate to display during a joyous fiftieth wedding anniversary celebration. But their absence from our friends' slide show underscores our tendency to idealize and romanticize marriage and our hesitation to speak forthrightly about the parallel journey of faith.

But how does a couple reveal personal, heartbreaking, or humiliating experiences without implying failure on the part of one or both partners? Even in today's tell-all environment, we are reluctant to admit that we have had or are having marital problems. Yet quarrels, misunderstandings, and crises disrupt every marriage. Our own responses were most likely typical; there were times when we wrung our hands or floundered helplessly, wept and railed and argued like noisy gongs and clanging cymbals, lapsed into periods of unrelenting and unforgiving silence, and more often than not, looked for blame in our spouse.

Anxiety, conflict, and despair—the fault lines of marriage—appear without warning. The loss of a job or unhappiness in the workplace may lead to financial problems and the erosion of self-esteem in the affected spouse. The arrival of the first child requires adjustments not foreseen by either parent. Coping with a large number of in-laws may overwhelm a spouse who comes from a small family. A serious illness or death in the family creates fears about death and dying for the first time. These are but a few of the scenes that bring on marital fatigue, the loss of intimacy, the drudgery of daily routine, and the frustration of seemingly endless and aimless drifting. The well of love and faith can quickly run dry.

In our experience, when spouses discover that their resources of faith are insufficient for their needs, they experience a deep yearning to find faith—faith in the institution of marriage, faith in each other's goodness and love, faith in a future together, and faith in God or a higher being. This is a pivotal moment when the need for what might be described as *faith aids* to restore, renew, and redirect the marital journey. Some couples turn to close friends or a trusted family member or mentor for help. Others seek direction from a counselor or health professional. Many will turn inward at first to find spiritual grounding and then seek a religious faith for nurturing. For some it will be a courageous first step to find and enter into a community of faith; for others it may be a return to the religion of their childhood or a church of another denomination.

The seeds of our own spiritual journey were probably planted well before marriage. In a recent article, writer and poet Kathleen Norris recalls that her own journey "began at age four, as a member of the 'cherub choir' of a Methodist church" (*Modern Maturity*, March/April 2001, p. 36). At fifteen, she turned away from the church as a source of spiritual sustenance; but in her thirties, when she realized "something had been missing" from her life, she found her way back, returning first to the church of her grandmother.

Like Norris, we, too, remember the faith of our childhood. Before his conversion to Christianity in college, Clifford subscribed to Buddhism, the religion of his immigrant parents from Japan. He remembers the Buddhist faith for its rituals and its importance as a center for the preservation of culture. Although he did not understand the *sutras* as they were chanted by the priest, he remembers the spiritual setting—the smell of incense, the clap-clap of wooden blocks, and the reverberating tones of the brass gong outside the building. His involvement with YMCA activities during college introduced him to Christian theology and influenced his decision to be baptized in a Congregational church near the university.

My journey began quite differently. My parents were Christians before their emigration from Korea to Hawaii. Methodist missionaries had opened schools in several Korean cities toward the end of the nineteenth century and converted many young people, especially women who were traditionally excluded from any formal education. I was "born" into the Korean Methodist Church in Honolulu, where services were bilingual. The sermons in Korean stretched endlessly, but the English version that followed was usually only a few minutes in duration. For many of us in the second generation, there was little to inspire us spiritually. But our parents seemed to find both joy and solace in their Christian faith. They had left a homeland subjugated by Japan at the turn of the twentieth century. Despite the hardships of immigrant life, Christianity offered them hope, freedom, and dignity. Even though I did not understand the words, I could sense the passion of the first generation during the reading of the scriptures or the singing of hymns. Seventy years later, I can hear the lilt of their voices in their fervent invocation of *Ha-na-nim*—God, the most holy.

For many years after our marriage, Clifford and I thought of ourselves as "closet" Christians. We attended weekly church services, sent our three children to Sunday school, supported the annual budget, and made pledges for the construction of new sanctuaries and educational buildings. We wrote checks for the hungry, the politically oppressed, and the poor in third world countries. But in the workplace and marketplaces, at community meetings, and in our conversations with friends and family, we said little about our faith and the need for spiritual grounding in our lives and in our marriage. There was a clear dichotomy between the spiritual and the secular.

In retrospect, we do not believe it was embarrassment or uneasiness of the sort that afflicts Americans today that made us silent about spiritual life. On paper we were "good" and loyal Christians, serving on church boards and commissions, advising youth groups and nursery school boards, and working on endless "social concerns." But even as we soldiered on, we had a growing sense that we were not rooted to our faith. Something was missing in our lives.

Perhaps our spiritual void was in part symptomatic of our generation's eagerness to embrace all the trappings of middle-class America, including a home, a car, a good job, children, and Sunday church services. Our Christian faith during the first years of our marriage now seems to have been more appearance than substance, more a longing for the good life than a yearning for spiritual fulfillment. We were married a decade after the end of World War II. We grew up during the Great Depression, reached adulthood during or just after the end of an epic world conflict, and entered the workplace during the mid-twentieth century—a time of economic uncertainty and international tensions. Our fathers were immigrants from Asia who initially worked as laborers on sugar plantations in Hawaii. Poverty, racism, prejudice, and struggles for upward mobility were not simply "issues" of social justice, but the realities of everyday living for them. They had high expectations that their children's lives as bona fide Americans would be easier and more fruitful than theirs had been.

On our quest to find the language of faith, we became church nomads, wandering from congregation to congregation, with a spiritual hunger we could not define. We kept saying to each other that we needed to find a minister who could "speak to us." Perhaps there was arrogance or a kind of intellectual elitism in this requirement. In contrast, most of our friends and family members seemed so content in their faith and in their loyalty to their congregations, Buddhist or Christian. But there was resentment on our part, too. We were members of a body of faith being asked to serve, to minister in the community, but who was ministering to us? Sometimes we were made to feel like "grownup Christians" who no longer needed nurturing in the faith.

There was also disappointment. During the late 1960s and 70s, more and more clergy were drawn to activism in social and political arenas. Their input and spiritual perspectives were undoubtedly valuable, but this public ministry demanded more time away from their flock. Perhaps we were old-fashioned, but we really looked to the pastor as a shepherd, one whose life and words gave spiritual grounding and direction to the flock, especially in times of crisis. And there were many times when we felt like proverbial lost sheep.

One of those times occurred when doctors discovered that our younger son had a severe curvature of the spine that would impair his lung function and ultimately cause heart failure. Without complicated surgery, the probability that he would survive past the age of thirty-nine was poor. But surgery carried a risk of permanent spinal paralysis. As our son left the doctor's office on the day he received the diagnosis, he looked up at the sky and cried out in the parking lot, "Why me?" We knew, of course, he was addressing God. It was a crisis of faith for all of us. We asked the senior pastor of our church for help. He said he would ask the youth minister to talk with our son. Sadly, there was a miscommunication, and no contact was ever made. Our own spiritual ground was shaky, but we turned to prayer and the reading of psalms for strength. The words of the psalmist, heard so often in the past, came back to haunt us:

> I lift up my eyes to the hills.
> From whence does my help come?
> My help comes from the LORD,
> who made heaven and earth. (Psalm 121:1-2 RSV)

We felt the presence of God as we looked each day toward the Koolau mountain range, that bulwark of earth, stone, and ironwood trees rising majestically over our island. The timely visit of an old friend, a pastor who had formerly lived in Hawaii, also sustained us. After hearing the news about our son, he said quietly, "One of the worst nightmares parents face is the moment when they realize that it's not in their power to take away their child's burden. But there is one thing they can do, and that is to stand with their child to give him strength." We understood then that even though we were walking "through the valley of the shadow of death," we were not alone on this journey; God would be with us at every turn. When our son took his first steps after surgery, we understood the meaning of spiritual joy.

Like our son, we, too, learned that illness is a metaphor, an "invitation" to open one's self to God. In the late 70s, I suddenly felt fatigued and barely able to walk up a flight of stairs. Tests revealed evidence of lead poisoning and damage to nerve endings. With months of recovery ahead, I felt spiritually bankrupt. It was a time of crisis for both body and soul. Even more unsettling, we were in another period of transition in church membership. A friend reminded me that the Chinese combine two characters to create the ideograph for "crisis"— one character stands for danger and the other, opportunity. For the first time in many years, I was given the luxury of time alone, space to think, meditate, write, and even dream. Years of tending to others —spouse, children, the community—of always being in someone else's orbit, had suspended my own needs for *spiritual* refreshment. My period of solitude would become a fallow field, a time for renewal of the spirit. With Clifford faithfully standing beside me, I learned to value the distance between spouses so eloquently described by German poet Rainer Maria Rilke:

> A good marriage is that in which each appoints the other guardian of his solitude. Once the realization is accepted that even between the closest human beings infinite distances continue to exist, a wonderful living side by side can grow up, if they succeed in loving the distance between them which makes it possible for each to see the other whole and against a wide sky. (*Letters to a Young Poet*)

When Clifford and I returned to church after a year's absence, it seemed fitting that the sermon on that day was entitled, "Homecoming." The language of faith began to take on new meaning. The epistle's words, "But you are a chosen race, a royal priesthood, a holy nation, God's own people" became less an example of Christian exclusivity and instead a call to Christian faith (1 Peter 2:9 RSV).

A decade later, Clifford suffered two debilitating illnesses; the first was a bout with cancer, followed a few years later by a heart attack and cardiac surgery. During our nomadic church years, he had become increasingly restive, wondering out loud if Buddhism might be more spiritually fulfilling. I wondered privately if this first illness might become the catalyst to return him to the religion of his childhood. But just as I had found peace in solitude, he, too, turned inward and began to read books about Christian faith and spiritual fulfillment. Friends came to our home and prayed with him. His fears about death began to recede; he had found his way back to the journey of faith.

Of course, illness is not the only test of faith in marriage. Any major crisis can precipitate a spiritual upheaval and destroy not only the sanctity of a marriage, but also the tenuous connections between husband and wife. According to recent statistics, one out of every two marriages in America will end in divorce. These are alarming numbers. But the recent proliferation of books on the spiritual life and journey reminds us that the search for spiritual fulfillment is hardly a unique adventure. The hunger is widespread; the church must respond.

At the beginning of our marriage, we were skeptical of the language of faith, but over time, sermons, prayers, the explication of scriptures, hymns, meditations, personal testimonies, and pastoral counseling brought us closer to spiritual fulfillment. Each crisis had led us to a dangerous precipice. It was only as we opened ourselves to the Spirit that we felt the power of words. Familiar scriptures have taken on new meanings. We now hear ourselves being "called by name." The ambiguities of faith have gradually receded. We are rooted in the faith at last, but our spiritual journey is not yet over. As the eminent preacher and educator, Howard Thurman, advised long ago, "There is a time of snow in all adventure."

11

Marriage and Worship

Karen M. and Howard W. Stone

You want to do *what?*"

That seemed to be the standard response when we first announced our engagement. We were eighteen and twenty years of age and ignorant of the difficulties that lay ahead. Nor did we know the high divorce statistics for teenage marriages.

We were in love, full of hope and excitement, and ready for an adventure. We had not worked out where to live, how to support ourselves, or how to pay for college. One relative sputtered that neither of us would ever graduate from college or amount to anything. "You'll probably end up divorced," he predicted ominously.

He was not very nice about it—but he was right. We probably *would* end up divorced. Now (in our late fifties), we can understand his concern although not his approach.

How did it all turn out? The story is not over yet, but thirty-eight years later we are still married. We are more in love, show more affection, like each other and our marriage more than ever.

That is not to say there were no ups and downs, that on occasion we did not emotionally beat each other up. There were, and we still do, though the occasions are now rare.

That is not to say there were no times when both of us wondered what we were doing in this relationship. We did, and sometimes still do. But when we smoothed out the bumps, marriage for us seems to have gotten better over the years. Mary G. Durkin described marriage as "not a smooth curve drawn on the chart of life. It is, rather, a series of cycles, of deaths and rebirth, of old endings and new beginnings, of falling in love again" (Andrew M. Greeley and Mary Greeley Durkin, *How to Save the Catholic Church* [New York: Viking Press, 1984], 126).

In this regard, marriage could be compared to foreign travel. The first trip to Italy on your own is difficult. The Italians do not much care for speaking English, the system of reserving seats on trains is mysterious, traffic is heavy, and the driving, well, frightening. By the sixth or seventh trip, there are still plenty more sights to see, discoveries to make, delicious dishes to sample, things that can go wrong. But it is safer and far more comfortable knowing what to expect on the highway, a few useful Italian words and phrases, how to order food and make a train reservation. Likewise, marriage still is an adventure, full of new discoveries and occasional pitfalls, though now we know the landscape better and can proceed with greater confidence.

How we would like to offer to readers the definitive answer, the essential how-to manual for our good fortune. Of course that would be impossible. What we can do, however, is comment on one element of our marriage that over the years has been a significant source of strength, a foundation that has centered it. That element is worship.

Vive la Difference

We are different people. Very, very different. While driving through the wheat fields of Kansas I (Howard) notice the quality of the crop, think in terms of so many bushels per acre; I (Karen) see the hues, the various textures, the movement of wind across the surface, and may not even know or care that it is wheat I am looking at. We operate differently. My motto (Howard) is "Do it yesterday," and I start working immediately to meet a deadline a long way off. My motto (Karen) is, "If you put it off long enough, you may not have to do it at all" and am energized by the last-minute rush to the deadline. I (Howard) roll the toothpaste up from the bottom and I (Karen) cannot figure out why it makes any difference to Howard. In temperament, we are poles apart. I (Howard) find misbehaving children to be annoying. I (Karen) make allowances for them. When Howard is doing the wash, I (Karen) want the clean laundry to be hung or folded just so; I (Howard) could not care less if the T-shirts are wrinkled.

We could fill a book with examples such as these, but perhaps you get the picture. In *The Intimate Marriage*, the authors suggest that a "considerable degree of emotional maturity is required to maintain a close relationship in spite of deep differences" (Howard Clinebell and Charlotte Clinebell, *The Intimate Marriage* [New York: Harper & Row, 1970], 183). We may not have quite the "considerable" maturity they suggest is required, but surely we have grown in appreciation of each other's differentness and in recognition of the positive resources each of us offers the union.

Growing Together

When you are very different people and your approaches to life are so divergent, something has to bind you together or it is easy to wander even farther apart until there is no relationship left. Over thirty-eight years of marriage, we certainly have grown together in a number of ways. We know how to play together and have kept on playing whenever possible, traveling the world and finding adventures close to home. We laugh at ourselves. Our interests, tastes, and beliefs are increasingly close if not identical.

I (Howard) have developed an appreciation for art (Karen's occupation), especially the applied arts. I enjoy living in the house decorated by Karen with early twentieth-century arts-and-crafts furniture, art deco items, and works of art. I even enjoy going to galleries, though art openings still drive me to distraction. I have followed her from church to church and art museum to gallery in Florence and Ravenna, Seville and London—though in London I generally abandon her and head for the Science Museum!

I (Karen) have learned to abide living in a house full of hundreds of vintage radios—no exaggeration—and to appreciate the pleasure Howard gets from restoring a mouse-infested old pile of junk to its original working condition. I still do not like the looks of big stereo speakers and thick cables lying along the floorboards, but I really enjoy listening to jazz and early music on the sound system Howard has built and assembled. I also have come to appreciate Howard's business and finance sense, especially as we approach retirement age. Although neither of us has been profligate with money, we have grown even closer on this issue. And I feel gratitude that Howard's thrift will help us to live comfortably in the final third of our lives. Meanwhile, I (Howard) have become more willing to spend money on things that we value, such as travel and aesthetics.

Joining in Worship

The humor, shared interests, and tolerance came with time. We always shared one thing: From the day we met as college students volunteering to start a Lutheran church in a suburb of Salt Lake City, through poverty in our student years and wobbly times in our relationship, through job changes, moves, parenting, and financial difficulties, even when the emotional love for each other was diminished, we have never lost the experience and the bond of worshiping together.

Worship assists in the honoring of differences. Will Willimon describes worship as "primarily a corporate and incorporating event, incorporating not only diverse people but also diverse traditions, expectations, expressions, and motives" (William H. Willimon, *Worship as Pastoral Care* [Nashville: Abingdon Press, 1979], 28). At Pentecost, many dissimilar peoples and traditions were brought into the church; today, ideally, worship still assimilates people with differences into the community. Corporate worship honors individuality, blesses mutuality, creates community. As Willimon puts it, "worship is always an integrative act of the community" (Willimon, *Worship as Pastoral Care,* 20). Worship therefore serves as an incorporating act in marriage and the family.

In worship, we do not lose ourselves but underline our individuality as well as our oneness in Christ. It is easy to become obsessed with problems in our lives and forget that we are part of a larger community. The liturgy reminds us whose we are and of our call to the priesthood of all believers.

Without fail, no matter what may have happened during the week, when it comes time for sharing the peace, we exchange a deep, long embrace and a blessing: "The peace of the Lord be with you."

Repeating the words of the liturgy Sunday after Sunday has a way of anchoring our lives and marriage not only at one point in time, but also on a continuum, as members of a vast communion of saints who for centuries have struggled with many of the same issues and repeated the same words. Just as the church has struggled, fallen into error, yet endured and renewed itself, the liturgy reminds us in our hardest times that there is hope, that our union can not only endure, but also continue to grow.

Praying together at mealtime, in worship, or at any other time, focuses our shared concerns. Some of our prayers are anguished. Some of them are whimsical. Some, like our favorite table graces, have been repeated thousands of times over the years. The repetition may offer up a precious memory, such as the time we sat at the table of a family in Denmark and learned their children's table grace: "Miel Alleluia, Amen!" to the tune of *Shave and a Haircut.* This grace is now a lighthearted favorite in our house and at the table of our daughter, son-in-law, and granddaughters.

The eating of a meal is a point of sharing in a marriage; it is not only for sustenance of the body but also functions as a mutual expression of love. We offer bread, a gift from God, to each other, and it becomes an expression of our communion with each other. Prayer at the meal reminds us of the gifts both of us have been given and the union we have in Christ.

Receiving the Eucharist side by side brings Christ's redemption to us as individuals and as a couple. It is healing and renewing. It also lets us know that sacrifice is not a dirty word. The sacrifice of Christ becomes a model for the sacrifice that any person in a long relationship is occasionally called upon to make: It is truly needed, freely offered (not demanded), and earns no reward. It does not debase or enslave the giver nor obligate the receiver. Perhaps those many years of sharing the Lord's Table have helped us become a little more gracious about the comparatively small sacrifices we make for each other.

Worshiping together on our travels has enriched those experiences, bound them to our faith, and provided dates and settings upon which to hang a memory. Evensong at King's College in Cambridge, where we lived during three sabbaticals, infused us with God's precious gift of beauty—beauty at this height having a spiritual power that binds us to each other at the moment and, later, in reminiscence. Christmas Eve was spent in a Guatemalan village church, fireworks popping outside the door, people shyly welcoming us and sharing God's peace with us in a language neither of us speaks very well. We have worshiped around a campfire, in a medieval cathedral, at a Mariachi mass in a San Antonio mission, in a simple country church, in the cave where Paul and Barnabus are supposed to have secretly worshiped in Antioch, at a storefront meeting room, sitting on planks under a baobab tree in South Africa, kneeling in a hospital chapel.

Several studies suggest that religious belief and practice correlate with satisfaction in marriage.[1] The benefit for marriages is measured by the degree to which religious practices inform and become a part of the relationship (Giblin, "Marital Spirituality," 322).

The Relationship Between Marriage and Worship

There is a natural relationship between marriage and worship. Elizabeth Achtemeier states that our Christian faith is, at its very core, about relationships. As she points out, "In the biblical faith, every family relationship affects the relationship with God, just as,

---

1. Paul R. Giblin, "Marital Spirituality: A Quantitative Study," *Journal of Religion and Health* 36, no. 4 (1997): 322; Paul R. Giblin, "Spirituality, Marriage, and Family," *The Family Journal* 4 (1996): 49ff.; Douglas A. Abbott, Margaret Berry, and William Meredith, "Religious Belief and Practice: A Potential Asset in Helping Families," *Family Relations* 39 (1996): 443; Layne A. Prest, Robin Russel, and Henry D'Souza, "Spirituality and Religion in Training, Practice, and Spiritual Development," *Journal of Family Therapy* 21 (1994): 74.

vice versa, God is at work in every area and relationship of family life" (Elizabeth Achtemeier, *Preaching About Family Relations* [Philadelphia: Westminster Press, 1987], 31). Indeed, at the dawning of Christianity, worship occurred only in homes. Unlike the rites of the mystery religions or the temple cultic acts of the Israelites, Christian worship began where people lived. It was a gathering of several households in the home of one of the members. Christians would assemble there to express their love and obedience to God. As German Martinez explains, "Houses were not only literally churches . . . but households give birth to communities. The worshiping community, as distinct from the sacred temple gathering, originated in the bosom of the family, around the table, and under the couple's hospitality" (German Martinez, "Marriage as Worship: A Theological Analogy," in *Perspectives on Marriage,* ed. Kjerin Scott and Michael Warren [New York: Oxford University Press, 1993], 95).

Every active family unit has its rituals—repeated acts and practices that are unique to the family. Every individual performs daily rituals, whether in rising, toilette, preparing food, eating, working, or praying. These rituals are natural to the way humans structure their existence. Martinez states, "Worship embodies an inner life, a belief through rituals, since the ritual is the cradle of religious belief. It has the proper language and external gestures of inner realities—as does a marital partnership" (Martinez, "Marriage as Worship," 83).

At one point in the historic Anglican wedding service, the bride and groom said, "With my body I thee worship" (James F. White, *Introduction to Christian Worship* [Nashville: Abingdon Press, 1981], 25). These words recognize that marriage calls for the total giving of one's self to the other in service and devotion. The same is true in worship. "True marriage, like true worship," writes Martinez, "is rooted primarily . . . in transcendent love. They both relate to something in the foundations of human consciousness and point beyond their reality. God is thus made present" (Martinez, "Marriage as Worship," 84).

The apostle Paul, frustrated by some of the problems and conflicts in the church at Corinth, reminded the members that the purpose of the church is to strengthen and edify its members. Willimon puts it this way: "One reason that worship is the center of the Christian community's upbuilding is that in worship, all the community's concerns meet and coalesce" (Willimon, *Worship as Pastoral Care,* 20). Worship mediates our lives, loves, and concerns with the life, love, and concerns of the Other. Worship mediates God for each of us individually and also as a couple. Confession and forgiveness, the Lord's Table, and prayer nourish and instruct us as individuals and as a family.

Growing in Grace Through Worship

We would love to say that we were wise children who recognized from the beginning that worship would be a key to anchoring our marriage. As it happened, the value of worship to our partnership dawned upon us slowly. But we always worshiped. We sat together, walked to the altar together, knelt together, took each other's hand, prayed together, sang in harmony, offered each other a blessing. Many times we have wept together when some theme of our faith struck a deep chord as it was acted out in the drama of the liturgy.

We believe it has been not the idea of worship but the cumulative *acts* of worship—the prayers, bread, wine, liturgy, music, art, and architecture and even the silence—that have worked upon us. Our differentness is safer, more tolerable, something even to enjoy and to celebrate, when anchored to the enduring traditions of our faith.

Just as worship is an act and a choice, our love for each other—in what we share and in our differences—is a choice we continue to make and an act that bears repeating.

12

God's Incredible Compliment

Don and Jean Shelby

God is never finished with us or with our world! This affirmation of biblical faith holds that not only "in the beginning" did God create the universe and human life and "saw that it was good," but also God continues to create and is at work in the midst of the events and upheavals of human history, effecting the divine purpose and making "all things new." While such divine activity and purpose are always surrounded by mystery, God gives us hints, signs, visions, and revelations.

For the Christian, God's greatest revelation is manifested in Jesus, in whom God wrapped up truth, whole-making love, and resurrection power for us and our world. When Jesus called people to share his mission, Jesus declared, "Follow me," which, translated literally, means "Come, walk with me along the road." Jesus also exhorted, "Be perfect [whole, complete], therefore, as your heavenly Father is perfect" (Matthew 5:48). In the Gospel of John, Jesus says, "I am the way, and the truth, and the life" (John 14:6).

Little wonder that the first Christians called themselves "Followers of the Way"—a felicitous naming. Later the apostle Paul would share with his friends in Philippi:

> Not that I have already obtained this or have already reached the goal; but I press on to make it my own, because Christ Jesus has made me his own. Beloved, I do not consider that I have made it my own; but this one thing I do: forgetting what lies behind and straining forward to what lies ahead, I press on toward the goal for the prize of the heavenly call of God in Christ Jesus. Let those of us then who are mature be of the same mind. (Philippians 3:12-15*a*)

Such scriptural assertions, corroborated in our own experience, make it plain why faith and life are best described as journeys. Both are perennial pilgrimages in which we are forever beginning again. The cost of a vital and strong religious faith is a continuous struggle to claim it, keep it, and share it. Spiritual maturity is always in process. We never reach the day when we can write down in our journals, "Today, I became mature" or "Now I have all the answers." On our way through life, and as we grow in faith, we are forever beginning. The poet Rainer Maria Rilke endorsed this when he wrote, "Don't you see that everything that happens becomes a beginning again and again?" He then added, "Could it not be *His* beginnings, since a beginning in itself is always so beautiful?" (Rainer Maria Rilke. *Letters to a Young Poet,* trans. Joan M. Burnham [San Rafael, Calif.: New World Library, 1992], 58). It has been so for us, for between faith coming alive in us and our coming alive in faith, there has been a journey—of horizons to be explored, not a few dead ends to be encountered, surprising arrivals and integrating certainties to be claimed and lived out.

Marriage also manifests this reality for us in a convincing way. Like most people who come to be married, we approached the marriage commitment and our wedding with the perception that because we loved each other so much, our marriage could not help being fulfilling, successful, and exemplary. But it was not long before we discovered that love is not some blissful state that people "fall into" and out of which emerges a perfect marriage. We have found instead that people learn to love each other through myriad events, experiences, impasses, misunderstandings, periods of estrangement, and conflict followed by reconciliation, efforts at communicating toward understanding, breakthroughs and openings, along with high moments of commitment, resonance, celebration, and laughter.

Moreover, marriages do not just happen. We create them as we explore wider dimensions of love and grow into deeper understanding of what being together means and requires. We shape, misshape, reshape, and hold on to our marriage relationship with courage, determination, and hope. The traditional liturgy of the wedding recognizes that marriages require effort in the question of intention put to the bride and groom. The question that is asked is not "*Do* you love . . . ?" but "*Will* you love . . . ?"

Love is volition and intention, as well as engulfing emotions, mutual need satisfaction, and reciprocity. Love is making promises and keeping them. Love is trust given and received. It is the commitment "to will the well-being of the whole being of each being, including one's own being, and thus to fulfill the will of the Supreme Being" as Bishop Melvin Wheatley once put it (Quoted from correspondence to Don Shelby from Bishop Melvin Wheatley, April 4, 2001). Love and marriage do not just happen, despite the fact that in both there is a dimension of spontaneity, serendipity, immediacy, and surprise. In a profound sense we make our marriages happen. And we then continue to revitalize them and keep working at them, especially during periods when we may not have the desire but do so because we have committed ourselves to stay faithful to our vow, to the commitment we have made to each other.

It is as amateurs that we grow into love and loving, and that is why we make mistakes, why we must learn more about who we ourselves are and who each other is, as well as explore what it means to be together, to share life, and to grow in intimacy, acceptance, loyalty, respect, and gratitude. The writer Kathleen Norris discovered that "true intimacy is frightening, and I was well into my marriage before I realized that I either had to seek it or live a lie. Intimacy is what *makes* a marriage" (Kathleen Norris, *The Cloister Walk* [New York: Riverhead Books, 1996], 108).

Growing into love and into loving, we learn that each of us is a mystery with a "shadow side," with tangled motives, hidden secrets, irrational urges, and streaks of confused emotions, which frighten us. Within each of us are guilty memories, neurotic hostilities, sexual frustrations, and unresolved contradictions. At times, such inner turmoil can break out in anger and wild threats—and unfortunately, in some marriages, the wild threats turn in to violent abuse.

Each person is an unfinished agenda. We may believe that as we enter into marriage we know each other well, but abruptly some facet in the personality of the other surfaces, forcing us to behold that person in an entirely different light. It is almost as if we are living with a stranger. Such moments can precipitate a crisis as we face accepting the revelation, talking with each other about how to resolve it, and deciding if we can accept this hidden attitude or repressed need as part of the person whom we love—or if that is impossible, seeking professional help and in some desperate circumstances, ending the marriage.

There are also the changing seasons of marriage that bring their unique challenges and pressures. If we become parents, we must cope with the responsibilities and changes that nurturing children brings: their needs in infancy, as they move through the preschool years, into elementary school, into adolescence, and later as they leave home. Couples who become parents must work through the stress that parenthood can bring to their marriage. Add to these the challenges brought by "midlife crises," "the empty nest," retirement, the deaths of parents, growing older and facing our own mortality, and we realize clearly how we are never finished, how we are forever beginning, how marriage is a journey we make. Included in the journey, we must add, are also the ecstasies that overwhelm us, the beautiful memories that we create, the sense of holy privilege we have in watching children grow and mature, and the moments of benediction that give us pause when we recognize what joy has been ours through it all.

Not only are people something of a mystery to one another; so also is life itself. There is so much that we do not know about the little that we do know. Life is made up of contradictions, dilemmas, ambiguities, and interruptions. That is why the apostle Paul said, "we see in a mirror, dimly" (1 Corinthians 13:12). To be sure, much of life is like seeing baffling reflections in a dark mirror, but we *do* see. There is always enough that we see to prompt us forward on the journey, but never enough to spare us making it, as George Buttrick suggested (*Sermons Preached in a University Church* [Nashville: Abingdon Press, 1959], 35). Life, love, and marriage are both risky ventures and risky adventures in which we are always creating and re-creating. We always exist in what Peter Bertocci called "a state of creative insecurity" (Peter Bertocci, *Religion as Creative Insecurity* [New York: Association Press, 1958], 94).

Such insecurity can give rise to anxiety and frustration, especially if we expect life to be free of problems and people to be perfect (which means we expect them to be what we need them to be). This reality may vex those who want always to be in control. For some people, such frustration and apprehension leads them to give up on love, to give up on marriage and their family.

What all of us need to understand is that while God created life with contingencies and contradictions, and while love and marriage require taking risks and giving up control, making compromises, and working hard at communicating with each other, we do not have to struggle or cope on our own. God, the Creator, draws near with divine love and invites us to be cocreators, offering us resources greater than our own upon which we can draw. We refer to this gift and promise as God's "incredible compliment."

In the first epistle of John are words that refer to this compliment:

> Beloved, let us love one another, because love is from God; everyone who loves is born of God and knows God. Whoever does not love does not know God, for God is love. God's love was revealed among us in this way: God sent his only Son into the world so that we might live through him. . . . No one has ever seen God; if we love one another, *God lives in us, and his love is perfected in us.* (1 John 4:7-10, emphasis added)

As we make our journey of faith and love, as we struggle and press on, God is at work in us, perfecting (completing, making whole)

108

our love, providing openings for us, and guiding us on our way.

Left only to our human resources, it is not possible to actualize the depth of love that creates and maintains fulfilling and lasting marriages. Limited in our vision, thwarted by sin, hampered by our fears and unresolved inner conflicts, we simply cannot deal with all the challenges and complex problems of two human beings living together in the intimate relationship of marriage. We need all the strength and wisdom we can claim, all the power to love with constancy that we can receive. God offers us such gifts by loving us alive in Christ, eliciting our better selves, calling forth our potential, and moving us to grow in greater trust and caring. By offering us such gifts, God bids us share in the miracle of cocreation. In a telling aphorism, Augustine underscored this "incredible compliment" when he wrote that "without God, we cannot; without us, God will not."

We quickly add that as we become cocreators with God, we do so with our human shortcomings, contentious ways, defensive posturing, and myopic way of seeing things. Our marriages, therefore, are subject to repeated misjudgments, doubts, moments of alienation, manipulation, and attempted exploitation.

Responding, however, to God's gracious invitation to be cocreators, we can face openly the obstacles and the differences between us, the mistakes we make, and the insensitive ways we respond, and find the way to move beyond them. God is with us as we work at conflict resolution and reach reconciliation, as we seek forgiveness and are willing to forgive. God will stay with us as we work at communicating on both a conceptual and an emotional level, learning each other's code so that messages between us are complete and bring us closer together. God will love us toward a constancy of love that keeps us together during the trying times of resolving differences, making adjustments, and picking up the pieces and starting over again.

With God's urging and help, we will also pursue greater intimacy, giving attention to what Howard and Charlotte Clinebell identified as the many facets of intimacy: intellectual intimacy, emotional intimacy, recreational intimacy, creative intimacy, aesthetic intimacy, conflict intimacy, crisis intimacy, commitment intimacy, and sexual intimacy (*The Intimate Marriage* [New York: Harper & Row, 1970], 28-31). We will strive not to neglect any type of intimacy, but to seek innovative and helpful ways to participate fully in all of them as much as we can.

A marriage that is exciting and fulfilling is one in which we ask for God's help in experiencing spiritual intimacy, which celebrates and enriches the other facets of intimacy. Spiritual intimacy emerges between us when we open ourselves to be made one (atonement) with the transcendent otherness of God and with the universe. Spiritual intimacy is the mutual awareness of God's near presence within and between us. It is the intuitive certainty that we are not alone in the universe, that what we experience in our love—in loving and being loved—is derivative of God's divine love. It is the intimacy that comes when we walk together through a shadowed valley and suddenly sense that we have been joined by Another and realize that it is Jesus walking beside us. Spiritual intimacy occurs when we are overcome with awe and wonder at the birth of a child, as we cradle the child in our arms, as we hold the tiny hand in our own or trace the sculpted lines of the child's ear. Such intimacy fills us as we stand silent together and watch a sunset or behold a wilderness vista from a mountaintop. We experience spiritual intimacy as we stand at the grave of one of our parents or as we keep vigil at the bedside of a longtime friend. We can share such intimacy as we kneel together in a candlelit sanctuary on Christmas Eve and receive Holy Communion, or stand on Easter morning and sing our resurrection faith, "Christ the Lord is risen today, Alleluia!" Spiritual intimacy also comes between us as we move beyond alienation and are reunited through reconciliation, as we forgive and are forgiven. It may come as, together, we take a stand against injustice and human oppression or welcome a stranger in need into our heart and into our home. In such moments it is almost as if we could reach out and touch the face of God.

As spiritual intimacy deepens between us, love becomes more than having our individual needs met, and becomes instead, as William Genne put it, "the overwhelming desire and persistent efforts of two persons to create for each other the conditions under which each can become the person God meant him [or her] to be" (Clinebell and Clinebell, *Intimate Marriage*, 196). Such spiritual intimacy is nurtured in a marriage as husband and wife pray together, worship together in a community of faith, and study the Bible together or with other believers in a small covenant group. Spiritual intimacy is nurtured also when in response to God's leading we reorder our priorities and engage in a ministry of servanthood at the crossroads of human need.

Our marriage began not only with the wonderful feelings of being in love and wanting to share life together, but also with wanting to be sure that our feelings and desires were part of God's will for us. As we talked about our marriage commitment, we both spent time in individual prayer and meditation as well as in prayer together. In the midst of our prayerful search, the answer came for Jean on a Sunday morning while she was worshiping in her home church in Ohio. As she stood to sing with the congregation the familiar hymn, "Praise to the Lord, the Almighty," and she came to the lines, "Hast thou not seen how thy desires have been granted in what he ordaineth," it was as if heaven opened and God said yes! The words of that hymn have remained powerful for both of us, speaking as they do of how God works in us, granting us our yearnings and desires as part of God's purpose and will for our lives. Through the forty-one years of our marriage, we have discovered how God has drawn us closer together and worked with us as we worked at our marriage, how in grace and love God has guided us on our journey and forgiven us when we strayed, and how God gives us tomorrow with resurrection hope in Jesus Christ. What an incredible compliment!

Some years ago in the December issue of *Life* magazine, there was featured a series of responses by a variety of well-known personalities in answer to the question, "What is the meaning of life?" Among the writers was Garrison Keillor, humorist, raconteur, and host of the popular radio program *Prairie Home Companion*. Keillor wrote in part:

> To know and to serve God, of course, is why we're here, a clear truth that, like the nose on your face, is near at hand and easily discernible but can make you dizzy if you try to focus on it hard.
> What keeps our faith cheerful is the extreme persistence of gentleness and humor. Gentleness is everywhere in daily life, a sign that faith rules through ordinary things: through cooking and small talk, through storytelling and making love, fishing, tending animals and sweet corn and flowers, through sports, music and books, raising kids—all the places where the gravy soaks in and grace shines through. (Garrison Keillor, "The Meaning of Life," *Life Magazine* 11, no. 14 [1988]: 82-83.)

God pays us an incredible compliment in inviting us to be cocreators of life, love, and marriage. We do not deserve the compliment, but we can be grateful for it by staying faithful at loving and being loved, following Jesus in what will always be a "soul-size" exploration, celebrating again and again those wonderful moments when "the gravy soaks in and grace shines through."

With an unknown member of the Johannine community in first-century Ephesus, we sing with joy the mystery of love:

> Beloved, let us love one another, because love is from God; everyone who loves is born of God and knows God. Whoever does not love does not know God for God is love. God's love was revealed among us in this way; God sent his only Son into the world that we might live through him. . . . No one has ever seen God; if we love one another, God lives in us and his love is perfected in us. (Raymond E. Brown, *The Epistles of John* [Garden City, N.Y.: Doubleday, 1982], 102)

13

Reflections on Marriage and the Spiritual Journey

Joan and Richard Hunt

In the beginning . . .

Ours was a joyous wedding in a working-class Methodist church, complete with families and friends from our church and community where we both grew up. Close friends celebrated our wedding then and have continued with us throughout the years. We had planned our exit from the wedding reception to avoid the pranks Joan's three teenage brothers hoped to pull. We waved to all as we entered our get-away automobile and discovered that Richard's wedding ring had fallen off his finger. After frantically searching and locating his ring in the street, we left. We surprised Joan's brothers by leaving our old Chevrolet at the scene and taking Richard's parents' new car on our honeymoon.

When we returned, Richard's dad noted that our car's headlights were very dim and that we should have them repaired. With closer inspection we discovered a wedding prank—thick wax on the lights, which we removed.

Warm memories of our special wedding are still part of our life together. Our preparation for marriage and our spiritual journeys began in our childhood families and continued through the years. When we talked and dreamed in the four years before our wedding, we visualized ourselves as a couple, holding hands, with Christ at the center of our marriage.

We begin with God and we end with God. Our life's journey is to grow into complete love for God and others—not because we are forced to, but because we chose to. We see marriage as a powerful relationship that either enables or negates this journey.

How marriage has led us to a deeper and enriched faith

Marriage is a metaphor of God's love for humans. The foundation for our marriage rests in the unconditional covenant God has made with us to continue to be faithful and reliable. This grace invites us to respond in loving and caring actions with confidence and integrity. We try to be like God in our daily marriage interactions.

Because God values us, we want to value others, beginning with each other and then our children, grandchildren, other relatives, friends, colleagues, neighbors, and others. Since God values us equally, we avoid a patriarchal or authoritarian marriage model, in which one partner tries to dominate the other. We continually seek to treat each other as friends, not as servants or slaves with one being controlled by the other. Jesus elevated his disciples to "friends" rather than "servants" or "slaves" (see John 15:12-17).

Our spiritual journey as individuals and our marriage journey are deeply intertwined. Both daily tasks and exciting peak experiences blend into a great symphony of love. Marriage informs and influences our spiritual formation as well as our physical, mental, and emotional formation. In marriage we seek to practice the presence of God (Brother Lawrence of the Resurrection, *The Practice of the Presence of God*, trans. Donald Attwater [New York: Phoenix Press, 1985]).

By God's grace, we try to take each other's perspective. We each realize that whatever I want from my spouse is also likely what my spouse wants to experience from me—such as acceptance, affirmation, and other support. If one of us is feeling lonely or rejected or hurt and wants love from the spouse, then it is very likely that the marriage partner is also having similar feelings. We welcome receiving each other's love, yet a continuing challenge is to reach out to the other in love rather than focus on our own needs. At times, we give grace to each other, and at other times receive grace. These are living expressions of scriptures such as 1 Corinthians 7 and Ephesians 5.

How marriage and the spiritual journey are related

We have not made sharp distinctions between the body, mind, emotions, and spirit in talking and in experiencing our spiritual journeys. We journey as whole persons—each dimension interacts with the others, and all have their place. The emphasis on system unity and diversity (Ephesians 4) applies to individuals, marriages, and families, as well as to churches and communities.

We are finding that each stage of life elicits its special perspective on God, making a "circle of life" as referenced in the recent movie, *The Lion King*. As children, we experienced enough safety, security, unconditional love, guidance, and nurturing from our parents and other caregivers to get us through adolescence to adulthood. Experiencing the many positives from our parents made it easy to begin to trust and love God, so we could transfer and expand our trust and faith to God as heavenly father, creator, and friend.

After several years of marriage, we became parents to two sons and discovered the joys and challenges of nurturing them to adulthood. This deepened our appreciation of God as giver and sustainer. Now, as grandparents, we observe the patterns, systems, and mutual exchanges in our adult sons' families. Our growing understanding of these families challenges us to give them freedom to find their own answers in life as we assure them of our unconditional love. Since we love them with our finite limitations, all the more we know that God loves us (Matthew 7:7-12).

It is as though God says to us, "You want to be God? You want to be in charge of the world? Okay, I'll give you the power to conceive and parent a few children to adulthood, then you can begin to know what it is like to be God." Through our experiences as children, spouses, parents, and grandparents, we understand better how God entices us to move from rules, laws, and commands to grace, relationships, and principles. In our marriage journey we continue to see, more clearly some times than others, the stages of faith and change so well described by Professor James Fowler (*Faithful Change: The Personal and Public Challenges of Postmodern Life* [Nashville: Abingdon Press, 1996]).

What direction might be offered to others who are struggling in their marriage?

Over our years together, five basic words have evolved to describe marriage for us. Based on 1 Corinthians 13, these dimensions are faith, hope, love, power, and joy. Our faith covenant means we will stay together unconditionally (thus, no divorce). Our vision for our future guides us as we love and care for each other as well as for family, community, and world. We seek to improve the skills and resources that empower us to enrich our marriage. Joy comes when we see positive results just as disappointment comes when things do not go as we want. Our dance among these five dimensions is intricately interwoven with our spiritual journey, with all of life. In our book *Growing*

Love in Christian Marriage (Nashville: Abingdon Press, 2001), we strongly encourage struggling couples to put God first in their marriage. To put God first means that both spouses see themselves and their marriage in relation to their total life commitment to God, the "something beyond themselves" who gives ultimate transcendent meaning to their lives and their marriage.

To put God first also means that "living happily ever after" takes commitment, work, and a willingness to change. Every couple will have conflicts and disappointments, yet successful couples take these as challenges to grow, not excuses to quit. When Jesus was asked about divorce, he pointed to God's original intent that through marriage, man and woman can enjoy life together (Mark 10:2-12). Jesus eliminated all excuses, noting that Moses allowed divorce for "hardness of heart" (unwillingness to love and forgive). The concession of Moses and of churches today is that divorce is better than murder, yet the invitation is to grow in love by responding to challenges. We hope that as a couple, and as churches, we are learning how to embody more love in our marriage. And we want every couple to catch this positive vision and grow so that they learn to stay together because they chose to stay together.

In marriage, the daily steps of one person elicit, like a dance, the responding step of the spouse. No matter what the situation, each spouse could have done something other than what they did. The exciting challenge is to grow by learning new positives to replace negatives in our spiritual journeys together.

At times, every couple needs encouragement and support from others. Make friends with other couples whose values are similar to your own. Get involved as couples in church community where you can do things together. Together we enjoyed our college's Methodist Student Movement, church camps, and couples fellowship groups that offered much support from friends with similar values.

Be open to whatever positive support you have from your family networks. Find good mentor couples who are willing to listen to you, share some of their own marriage challenges, and introduce you to others who have specific help for your situation. You find these types of friends by being so involved in a church fellowship that each week you both just assume that you will go to church and participate rather than argue about whether to go.

Putting God first also implies that every couple needs to agree on basics that form the foundation for their mutual love. Your covenant to stay together happily for the long term both brings fun (joy) and requires work. At times, each spouse needs to compromise or give in on lesser issues in order to achieve bigger lifetime goals. After all, maybe how you load the dishwasher or squeeze the toothpaste tube is not as important as enjoying romantic times with each other. By grace, God accepts us as we are, so we can accept each person as she or he is. Your spouse is just about as perfect or imperfect as you are.

There are some very basic lifestyle decisions every couple must make. Stated negatively, they include no hitting or hurting your spouse, no disrespect, no putdowns of each other. Put positively, you need to create caring days and habits that fill your marriage with enjoyable experiences. Every day give a hug and affirmations to your spouse.

What do you think are the keys to a happy marriage?

We think the best Christian model for marriage is an interactive system of mutual regard—a community of grace and unconditional love that is centered in the trust of both spouses in God as Father, Son, and Holy Spirit. This "common-union" is our communion with God and each other.

In some weddings, there are two candles to represent the husband and wife. Then these candles are used to light another candle to represent the marriage. Unfortunately in some services, the first candles are extinguished; but when married, we create a new family as well as continue to be individuals in our marriage, as parents, and with our families and friends.

If you want to change your spouse, begin by changing yourself. Decide what you want your spouse to do, then do that yourself. For example, if you want your spouse to be more patient, first be more patient yourself. Be clear about what you want, then check with your partner to see if she or he sees your changed behavior in the way you intended.

Any situation—good or bad—took a long time to get that way, so changing it will also take determination and time. The explosive demolition of a building appears quick, but it takes careful preparation, the weakening of the structure, and then the final explosion.

Learn from mistakes. Ask what can we do differently to accomplish our positive goals.

Temptations occur because a person has not fully committed to his or her spouse and marriage. Usually thought of as bad, temptations can be an opportunity to grow. What appears to be desirable in the short run may not be so in the long run, once it is experienced.

Faith's importance in our marriage

Throughout our marriage, faith has been fundamental in several ways. Faith refers to our own personal spiritual beliefs and experiences, to our participation in a community of many somewhat like-minded persons, and to our commitments to healthy values and behavior patterns.

1. Our own personal spiritual beliefs and experiences include "peak experiences" of feeling especially close to God through family celebrations. Spiritual growth experiences include discovering the bigger picture of God's creation through science, art, and nature, as well as finding answers to prayers. We continue to explore big questions, such as why God created the universe, world, and us; how this life relates to life eternal; and meanings, choices, and "coincidences." We equally enjoy the small questions such as why every leaf is just a bit different and why children become so excited about discovering anything and everything. We have even explored why Richard's grandmother always hung her long hose as her Christmas stocking when Richard, at age three, had only his tiny sock—a comparison he still thinks was somewhat unfair!

Faith and hope give us a long-term life perspective. A few years ago we collected all home movies we had of birthdays, Christmas, other family events. In these we have movies of our sons at each age (from one to about fifteen years old), their grandparents, and relatives (some of whom are no longer living). We combined these into one narrated videotape of our family and gave it to our sons and their families at Christmas. It is a delightful treasure of family history. It gives our daughters-in-law and our grandchildren an opportunity to see their great-grandparents and other relatives, as well as to confirm that their own fathers were once children (sometimes hard to believe). Since then, Joan's family has compiled a videotape history of photographs and other materials that adds to the richness of our family heritage.

2. Participation in a community of somewhat like-minded persons expands our friendships and anchors us with others. In our journey, we have always been involved in the life of a local church, especially in a fellowship class of couples and individuals. Sometimes that community disappoints us, yet many more times our church involvement stabilizes us. Our typical Sunday morning question is not, *Shall we go to church this Sunday?* but rather, *What can we accomplish through our friendships and worship at church?*

We have also found friends, mentors, and supportive persons

through our work, neighborhood, and other networks. At times professional colleagues and neighbors have offered advice and assistance and have given us opportunities that we would not have otherwise found. We have tried to reciprocate by being available to others as opportunities arise. Because others have cared for us, we now try to care for others—a theme in the movie *Pay It Forward* as well as in 1 John 4:7-20.

3. Our commitment to healthy values and behavior patterns points to trying to implement the best that we know in our daily interactions. Since the only way to know another person is through observing and experiencing his or her behaviors, it is essential that we act in ways that really express who we are. In the mystery of interpersonal relationships we also discover God's presence (Matthew 18:20). When things go right, we then know what to do again. When things go wrong, we try to troubleshoot the pattern to find what we can to do differently and better the next time.

An especially important time for us is our daily "re-entry" time when we return home from work, school, or volunteer activities. When our two sons were in elementary school, Richard would come home, change clothes, and then play with the boys to give Joan some free time and to have some "father and son" time with them. Joan saw the value of the relationship between father and sons and often purposely waited to begin meals until Richard got home. It was wonderful that each of us felt confident of the other's trust and thus did not need to worry about being left out when the other parent was alone with the children. As parents, we tried not make any policy decision about a child without first talking with each other. This supported us as a family and prevented any parents-child triangles that left out the other parent. Having a secure support base in our spouse helped us believe in each other and gave encouragement and perspective.

Marriage nourishment is like making deposits in an emotional bank account. Regular deposits are essential in order to have a balance of resources from which to draw needed support. We recommitted many times across our various stages of life.

Our family has been blessed with good health, positive career and educational opportunities, and moderate financial security. This gave us a context for coping with stress and crises, such as Richard's prostate surgery and follow-up radiation. Adjustments to change have deepened love and expanded possibilities for caring for each other. Richard's eye lenses implant surgeries not only gave him renewed vision, but also have become a metaphor for the focus and clarity of vision that brings renewal in marriage and new expressions of spirituality.

Have your marital satisfaction, happiness, tolerance, and adjustment increased or decreased during the time you've been married?

Marital joy, satisfaction, and happiness is a day-to-day affair, not just a matter of "living happily ever after." Our marriage joys increase when we are intentional and organize time for ourselves, as a couple, our family, the community, and the church. Happiness and joy may be different in each life stage. There are the special joys that have come as we graduated (several times), moved, purchased our first new car, bought a house, later built a new house, and budgeted for savings.

Two major components in marital satisfaction are change and accommodation. These involve negotiations among marriage, career needs, children, and the many changes as children grow and eventually leave to form their own homes. As is pointed out in the serenity prayer, we can change some things but must adjust to those things we cannot change.

Like all couples, we have made many adjustments and compromises, establishing our own family patterns while integrating each of our families' heritages. One humorous example of early marriage compromise is the matter of what constitutes "real" strawberry shortcake. Joan's family always had a flat piecrust type of cake and added strawberries just before eating so it did not get too soggy. Richard's family's shortcake was a yellow cake with strawberries added early enough to allow the cake to get soaked with juice. After several discussions about "proper" strawberry shortcakes, we compromised that each style is different, yet good in its own way.

Many of our marriage joys are in doing things together. Now, as grandparents, we see more of the effects of lifelong family patterns and the results of modeling in our grandchildren. We are so glad to be together to share in the family events.

How have we related our spiritual journey in our marriage to our careers, children, church, and society?

We have learned through our faith that forgiveness is an essential component in a successful marriage. In times of disagreement, anger, or conflict, from our long-term faith view, we know that "this, too, will pass." Some matters we may never resolve or accept, yet none of these will keep us apart. We will always come back together, to reset our relationship with understanding and love.

Forgiveness is our "reset button" because it allows each of us to offer love and care, regardless of how messy a situation may have become. Forgiveness is saying, "It doesn't matter whose fault it is. The important goal is deciding how we will live from this point forward."

We know that we are never alone. Through prayer and through many other experiences, God continually invites us to grow in love. After we have done our best, we leave it in God's hands. Often we have knocked on a door that does not open, but another even better opportunity does open. Rather than attributing this to "coincidence," we see (often in hindsight) God's involvement in the situation.

We model our marriage covenant on God's unconditional covenant with us (Joseph L. Allen, *Love and Conflict: A Covenantal Model of Christian Ethics* [Lanham, Md.: University Press of America, 1995]). Just as a tree with strong roots and flexibility can withstand winds and storms, so our commitment is rooted in our faith. Changes in our careers, children, church, and society interact with changes in our marriage, yet our fundamental relationship is with each other before God. In many ways our faith has made our marital journey more confident and joyous.

14

Marriage As Sacrament and Covenant

Patrick and Kathleen DeSutter Jordan

After nearly thirty years of marriage, we can say with unhesitating hearts: We continue to grow in love each day. That, of course, is a grace, not an achievement. Still, at this particular moment in cultural history, it is an all the more rare, if unmerited, accomplishment. It is also the result of hard work: of mutual candor, attention, a shared life of faith, and the effort to ever deepen our affection.

Since this is the first time we have been asked to write about marriage, we will necessarily be autobiographical. In choosing such an approach, therefore, be warned: By most standards, we are simultaneously peculiar and rather uninteresting. That is, we are so regular and mundane as to be boring but so atypical, by present standards, as to be of little practical help to almost anyone else.

We met on a picket line in the fall of 1969. Although we had worked together for several months at the Catholic Worker in New York City, we had never really talked. The Catholic Worker was located near Manhattan's Bowery in a depressed neighborhood and offered hospitality, food, and clothing to anyone in need. Peter Maurin and Dorothy Day, two lay Catholics who had a radical vision of how to re-create society along Christian lines, had founded it in 1933. Voluntary poverty and pacifism are central tenets of the movement.

That fall, the United Farm Workers were protesting outside the Veterans' Affairs building on Seventh Avenue. The picketers were objecting to the policy of the Nixon Administration, which was digging the country deeper into the Vietnam quagmire. Furthermore, the government was attempting to break the UFW's boycott of scab grapes by purchasing huge quantities and shipping them in the form of fruit cocktail to our soldiers in Vietnam. As we marched the protest line together—both in our mid-twenties, both the children of middle-class Catholic families, and having spent years in formation as members of

Catholic religious communities—we found that we had independently arrived at the Catholic Worker with the same hope of deepening our Christian lives in the midst of the chaotic political and theological epoch. Not that we understood all this at the time, but it *was* exciting.

Dorothy Day was in her early seventies then. (Maurin had died in 1949.) A valiant and still vital woman, she became our mentor and friend. We worked at Saint Joseph House on First Street, sharing a life of simplicity (necessities, but no pay), protest, and war resistance, and doing the works of mercy. We helped cook meals, fight off bedbugs, visit the imprisoned, bury the dead, beg for food, and edit and distribute the *Catholic Worker* newspaper. In sum, we were thrust into a place where we could learn about Christian nonviolence and the need for creating an entirely different kind of society: one at cross purposes with both American capitalism and Soviet-style communism, one pointing toward service and cooperation, based on the gospel ethic of Christlike justice and compassion.

A remarkable thing about the Catholic Worker is that, by and large, it is a community of equals. There is little distinction between those who are drawn to help and those who need assistance. The common experience is that those who help are the ones who are helped the most—a gloss, perhaps, on Jesus' confounding words that those who already have will be given more. And so it was and is.

But there was also equality in work, in gender responsibilities, and in leadership roles. Men and women worked side by side at the same tasks, from scrubbing bathrooms to editing the newspaper, and attained positions of trust and authority by dint of their dedication, talents, and earned acceptance on the part of others. For us, the Catholic Worker was the association in the common work of offering hospitality, little by little creating a new vision of society, and daily attempting to grow in the life of the spirit.

Little did we know at the time, but such a community and such a shared experience was also a unique school for meeting an eligible partner. And it was a remarkable testing ground. A Catholic Worker house is something of a social crucible, one that specializes in the encounter with the human condition *in extremis*. Not only do the poverty and the filth, but also the violence, the addiction, and the mental imbalances that can breed in America's skid rows, march through its doors. If you want to know someone's real mettle, observe him or her in such a setting, day in and day out. Can this person cope? Does he or she have a sense of humor? What drives that person? Can you trust him or her with your life? Is his or her love genuine? Do you get along?

As we said, our meeting and coming to know each other in this place was a grace. For us, the Catholic Worker was a school in the cost of discipleship, a theological graduate school of sorts with the most remarkable curriculum, instructors, and practicum: a community of individuals and ideals that made Christianity and Christ vibrantly alive.

So we walked on the picket line together, talked, and found that we had more in common than washing dishes or begging for Friday's supper at the Fulton Fish Market. There were music (we went to hear Richie Havens at the Fillmore East and *La Bohème* in Central Park), baseball (Kathleen once completed an unassisted triple play at a Catholic Worker picnic), theology (Kathleen had studied Scripture under Carroll Stuhlmueller and Walter Brueggemann, Pat under Joachim Jeremias), and war resistance. Finally, or perhaps first in line, there was physical attraction. That we made it to our marriage bed as virgins, we readily admit, was only by God's doing. We would take long walks together, hand in hand, stride for stride, and still do. And by God's design, eventually everything seemed to fit.

"Don't get married until you *have* to" was Dorothy Day's message to us. Of course, she was not recommending a shotgun marriage; she meant, rather, "Don't jump in until you are absolutely sure." That advice, taken to heart, made for a relatively long, three-year courtship. It seemed even longer, since we were together for dramatic, exhausting stretches of work. Our companionship was not restricted to dates or weekends. We were together most of the week and were excited by the very notion of seeing each other—as when that remarkable someone walks into a crowded room and all the hairs on the back of your neck stand up. It happened repeatedly.

But, as we said, it was wartime. There were frequent protests, and Pat was arrested outside the White House. In jail, a fellow protester told him about Pendle Hill, the Quaker study center near Philadelphia that offered courses in nonviolence. Pat applied and was given a scholarship. The following spring, Kathleen received a working scholarship, and for eight weeks in an idyllic setting—beautiful grounds, remarkable teachers, un-Catholic Worker-like food—we had the chance just to be with each other. We studied the tales of the Hasidim with Eugenia and Maurice Friedman and read Martin Buber's *I and Thou* together. But at the end of our time there, instead of being ready to walk down the aisle, we seemed further from it. Sensing that there were still elemental personal issues to be faced, we decided to part as friends—with broken hearts.

That fall, Pat was arrested, tried, and convicted on two counts of draft resistance. But at his sentencing, the judge—who was known as a hanging judge—directed that Pat be remanded to the Catholic Worker. Instead of the anticipated separation, we were back at work together and, with time and rediscovery, back in love. Long conversations, greater maturity, and learned patience bore fruit. On August 15, the Feast of the Assumption, 1972, we attended afternoon Mass together. Because of a confluence of the scripture readings, the homily, and the Sacrament, when we walked out of the church, we proposed to each other. When we told Dorothy Day the following morning, she remarked, "I thought he'd *never* ask."

At the heart of the Catholic idea of marriage, and what gives it its texture, brilliance, and durability, are two essential notions: sacrament and covenant.

Covenant is rooted in the Hebrew word *berith*: a formalized, legally binding agreement or contract that may exist on the individual, communal, social, or spiritual levels. It is God's covenant with Israel that binds God and Abraham's descendants forever. It is the blood of the New Covenant that brings us the fullness of redemption.

God's promise is not only eternal and redemptive, faithful and faith giving, but also full of *hesed*, that is, steadfast love. Walter Brueggemann writes that in the positive descriptive adjectives applied to Yahweh in Exodus 34, *hesed* is the only word used more than once, indicating that this particular aspect of God's character receives special accentuation (Walter Brueggemann, *Theology of the Old Testament* [Minneapolis: Fortress Press, 1997]).

It is this revelation of God's Being as faithful and compassionate that is central to the poetic rendering of the divine character found in the book of Hosea. There, we are told, God will remain forever loyal, loving, and forgiving—in spite of everything. And because of this, we in turn must learn to be faithful and merciful.

The Catholic idea of sacrament, on the other hand, is essential to any understanding and practice of Catholic Christianity. In sacrament, the corporeal (human and concrete) and the divine meet and are sealed; the created and the creator intertwine in a salvific event. Sacrament is an evolving notion, yet it is the golden string that runs through the ancient, ongoing tradition of the church and is thus a constitutive aspect of being and becoming "Catholic" (See Keenan B. Osborne, *Christian Sacraments in a Postmodern World: A Theology for the Third Millennium* [New York: Paulist Press, 1999]).

Martin Buber has written that the foremost meaning of sacrament is that the divine and the human join themselves in each other and that this binding is in itself an act of covenant: "The covenant of the Absolute with the concrete takes place in sacrament" (*Theology of the Old Testament* [New York: Philosophical Library, 1948]). In marriage, he notes, a man and a woman consecrate themselves sacramentally, and simultaneously the covenant with the Absolute is consummated. Thus the consecration affected by the marriage vows is produced not by the power of the human partners alone, but by the strength and presence of the Absolute who blesses and unites them. Vows are said, therefore, not only to each other or even to the community, but also to God.

The sacrament of marriage is furthermore modeled on Christ's irrevocable covenant of love for the church (Ephesians 5:32). In the last century, the Catholic Church emphasized this teaching in the documents of the Second Vatican Council (particularly *Lumen gentium* [11] and *Gaudiun et spes* [48], and in the *Catechism of the Catholic Church* [1623 ff.]). In these statements, the church movingly underscored the sacramental and communal bond and how it is enhanced in the practical, daily lives of spouses. The family is described as a "school for humanity," indicating that spouses have a responsibility toward the wider community and society in general. In the Latin Church, spouses, rather than the priest, are the ministers of the sacrament. They confer it on each other before the church, represented by the priest and other witnesses. The act of making love confirms the spouses' mutual free consent, binding them to each other before God and all creation.

We were married on a hot September evening, on a school night, and Kathleen had to attend nursing classes the next day. We had composed the service within the framework of the Catholic liturgy but embellished it somewhat with elements from the Quaker wedding ceremony—our vows were spoken out of a reflective silence that followed a series of readings. Before the final blessing at the Mass, these vows were proclaimed from a scroll on which they had been recorded. The scroll was then signed by all present as witnesses. It hangs in an honored place in our bedroom.

The readings included a long meditation on love and service as found in the Hasidic tradition, the parables of the Kingdom in Mark and Matthew, and finally a reading from Hosea 2, which immediately preceded our exchange of vows. The vows themselves, based on verses 19 and 20, were as follows:

Dear Kathleen (Patrick), asking the blessing of the Lord, and your own, and in the witness of these our friends, I ask you now and I promise this day to betroth you to me forever; to betroth you to me in steadfast love and in mercy; to betroth you to me in faithfulness all the days of my life.

These words of promise and pledge have served us well. They have been a perennial, and often daily, inspiration and challenge. They have called and recalled us to love each other with the mercy, patience, forgiveness, and faithfulness of the living God. While at times and for long stretches they have been difficult to honor and live up to, their challenge has been a life spring, a source of renewal, and a searing call to conscience.

Our rings were simple gold bands provided by the Catholic Worker. Inside they are inscribed with the Hebrew word *berith*, "covenant," reminding us of God's faithfulness and loving-kindness.

After the Eucharistic Prayer and Communion, there was an exchange of gifts: a copy of the Scriptures, a crucifix that hangs over our bed, and a traditional Hebrew prayer shawl, its blue and white colors signifying purity and fidelity. This was placed around our shoulders, binding us together, as we led the assembly in singing the Magnificat.

Afterward, everyone joined us at our apartment for a Catholic Worker feast: roast beef sandwiches on homemade bread and a homemade cake. In some very real sense, time stopped that night, and we entered a special realm. We still remember the presence of each other that evening, the glow, and in recalling it, we are renewed. We have no question that God was there and blessed us. We know it still in each other's kiss, in the pressed hand, in the acts of love, and especially in each other's forgiveness and joy.

We were practicing Catholics, married in the aftermath of the 1968 papal encyclical *Humanae vitae*—Pope Paul VI's reaffirmation outlawing artificial birth control—and our married life has been a daily experience of the theological and moral whipsaw that was set in motion by that pronouncement. Against our common reason and intuition, we have nonetheless attempted to govern our sexual life in accord with the church's proclaimed teaching, which has proved time and again to be a physical and spiritual cross, and one that has seemed almost totally unredemptive.

From our own vantage point, we have experienced that the church's approved "natural family planning" methods not only seem unnatural but also exaggerate the tensions already inherent in attempting to maintain and enhance a loving, monogamous relationship in a highly sexualized and overstimulated culture. If the teachers of the official church were to ask us, we would say that while we aspire to the ideals of *Humanae vitae*, we think the hierarchy's teaching is flawed and counterproductive. That we continue to try to live by it brings a sense of bemusement even to ourselves. Still, this attempt stems from our love for the church and its people and our desire to submit our wills to the will of God.

God has blessed us with two fine children, food for the table, legitimate and often rewarding work, many friendships, and available communities of prayer. For the first ten years of our married life, we subsisted below a taxable income in order to refrain from directly contributing to arms production and nuclear war preparations. The benefits of this decision were many: a life of simplicity and a great deal of time with our growing children. Eventually, we had to bite the bullet and pay the taxes, as we could no longer afford to provide for their education without taking home a larger salary. We have found that marriage is the hardest work in our life, and conversely the most liberating. We have learned the importance of candor and of sensitivity, and how they must be balanced and apportioned. We have learned that there are long seasons when love and affection seem unrequited and unfulfilled. We have learned patience and that the antidotes are hope, forgiveness, and more patience. But the longer we have been married, no matter the trials, the more delicious it has become.

In the early years of our marriage, Dorothy Day would often quote to us Catherine of Siena: "All the way to heaven is heaven"; Dostoevsky: "Beauty will save the world"; and John of the Cross: "Where there is no love, put love, and you will find love." From such teachers we have learned that God's ways are trustworthy and worth every effort to comply with. Coupled with the sense of the cross being at the heart of human life and redemption, these phrases have become our touchstones. In all honesty, we are happier today than we have ever been, and we are still only on the way.

15

Happily Uncharted

Diane Kenney and DarEll T. Weist

We began dating in 1984. Very early in the relationship, Diane asked a question subsequently found to be of importance. "Why," she asked DarEll, "are your African masks and other artifacts packed up in the garage? Why are they not displayed in your house?" The question surprised him. What really startled him, though, was that he did not have an answer.

What was the source of these masks? After serving a three-year term in Sierra Leone as a theological teacher in the early 1970s, DarEll, his wife, and their two children returned to the United States, where their lives continued in patterns they had developed prior to their African experience. Slowly the family situation changed, and a divorce occurred. DarEll continued to apply his administrative and theological skills in various appointments within denominational structures. What Diane's question triggered was a realization that he had not fully incorporated the African experience into his theology. He had not examined how his spirituality had been affected by African students, by his new understanding of African historic religions, and by African Christianity. Slowly the boxes were unpacked and the integration began. Bringing those masks and other artifacts into what was now "his" house was like greeting old friends. It caused him to think and work through, once again, who and what God is for him.

Shortly after, Diane was invited to join a small group traveling to Nicaragua for the Nicaraguan and U.S. presidential elections. Her initial response to the invitation was that she could not possibly afford it. DarEll's question was, "How can you afford not to go?" Part of Diane's spiritual life had been forged in the demonstrations of the United Farm Workers movement in California as she completed a theological degree in Berkeley. Subsequent campus ministry work in the

Bay Area meant involvement in antiwar efforts. A move to a campus ministry position in Youngstown, Ohio, introduced her to a steelworker society decimated by corporate shutdowns. The Nicaragua trip would affirm her religious understanding of social justice as she stood with others observing the U.S. government's involvement in that country's civil war.

It is out of the questioning of each other that our marriage enriches the spirituality of the other. Our life together has developed into an ongoing dialogue, one that deepens and enriches the faith of the other.

Some of our better friends think we have little in common. A very close friend of DarEll's could not understand his interest in marrying "such a feminist." A valued friend of Diane's called her the day of the wedding just to make certain she "knew what she was doing," and then to offer her blessing. The commonalities most evident are that both of us are middle-class Caucasians, ordained (but in different denominations), have had extensive ecumenical and interfaith experience, are members of the same generation, and are inquisitive.

If we were to define our individual and collective faith journeys during these sixteen years of marriage, we would label it as "happily uncharted." Spiritual directors and psychological counselors are our friends, but we have not engaged them professionally. We often say that the funds others spend on spiritual direction, we spend on travel.

DarEll has counted some fifty countries we have visited independently or together. Diane never gets around to making lists. Our dilemma is, we have encountered so many places we value that we struggle with whether to return to a place for additional involvement in a particular culture or to try "someplace new." Despite this struggle, the spiritual dialogue continues. Seldom do we pray or read scripture together. Our vocations and ordinations mean that we are in separate parishes most Sunday mornings. Working on our individual and collective faith journeys is a constant process of conversation. Questions, reflection, and new insights are always on the agenda.

We speak of traveling, and we do travel often. However, the same engagement results from seeing a film or hearing a concert or even overhearing someone else's dinner conversation. A discussion about a "Sweet Honey in the Rock" concert might go on for days as we consider what leadership means in that cooperative group and might mean in the groups with which we work, question each other about what a particular phrase engendered, and discuss the ways truth can be learned in music. One evening in a restaurant, those around us might have assumed we were longtime "marrieds" who no longer had anything to say to each other. The reality was that we had individually tuned in on the conversation of the three gay men seated at the next table. All appeared to be in their early forties. Two were longtime residents of the community (we found out by listening in). The third had just moved closer and was being introduced to the area. They were competent, creative, and currently single. All were property owners. Their conversation finally focused on not yet being fully accepted by their parents. Individually we considered the uncountable hours the denominations of which we are a part have spent distracted by and struggling with whether gays and lesbians are to be fully welcomed. That night, we talked between ourselves about evil as a force that feeds on fear, a force that worms its way in, divides, sidetracks, and keeps humans from building genuine community.

Several years ago, we spent a month in a continuing education course in Israel. The subject was the liturgy of the Eastern and Western churches, and the course took place during the Lenten and Easter seasons. Diane, who considers liturgy one of her specialties, was delighted. DarEll, who did the research and discovered the course, comes from a more evangelical background and says he "learned a lot." One of the spiritual benefits of the course was encountering an icon of Sophia. Diane had asked one of the course leaders if he had ever seen a Sophia icon in Jerusalem. He had not but promised to continue looking. One day the leader returned from the Old City, telling us of a new discovery and urging us to visit the icon in a particular shop on the Via dela Rosa. We went to look at it. It had been a Russian family icon. The fun began! The dealer hoped he was encountering some rich Americans and told us Sophia could be ours for a mere $10,000 U.S. If we were hesitant, then we "would need to spend time with her, to see if she spoke to us." He invited us to take the icon back to campus for the weekend. We did take her, wondering about this culture where we were not even required to sign for such a valuable object. Sophia did speak to us, but not in ways that caused us to purchase her. She spoke to us about the need for wisdom, a wisdom so often replaced by rules, categories, and votes within our individual denominations. She spoke to us of academic integrity and spiritual discernment. She spoke to us of the time one must take to understand oneself and another. A photographic copy of the Sophia icon is displayed in our common office, and she continues to remind us of the need for wisdom in the process of our own faith development and in our professional work with others.

As a part of the same sabbatical, we were in Rangoon at the central

Buddhist temple. We had toured the facilities and observed many lay and religious persons making their offerings at the various statues of Buddha. It was difficult for us to understand this spiritual exercise. To our uneducated eyes, it appeared as if many were asking Buddha for favors, for the gift of good health or good fortune (not so different from many forms of Christianity). So we wandered, respecting the rituals, watching closely, and occasionally discussing what we were seeing. Suddenly a very British voice called out to us. We turned to face a saffron-robed monk with a bright smile. Remember that this was in Myanmar (formerly Burma), where nationals are not to talk with Westerners. We were accompanied by a government tour guide in all our wanderings. We understood from our reading (and subsequently from the guide) that governmental spies were everywhere. One needed to be careful because one never knew who might be listening. We did not fear for ourselves (U.S. citizenship provides considerable protection), but we are always careful not to intentionally endanger others. This Buddhist monk began asking us questions: "Where are you from?" "The U.S." "Where in the U.S.?" "California." "Where in California?" He had never been to California, but he had visited other parts of the United States during a gentler time in Myanmar's history. He had befriended a former U.S. ambassador and obtained much of his reading material from Jesuits previously working in the country. We told him we were both clergy. He took Diane's hand, saying "A woman minister! I've never met one!" Diane handed him her card. It was only later that Diane read in a travel guide that under no circumstances was a woman ever to touch a Buddhist monk.

The monk discovered that DarEll was a United Methodist, and then *he* told us all about John Wesley. Our tour guide was very uneasy with the conversation and tried to move us along. The monk's final question was, "I have been reading Noam Chomsky. What do you think of him?" In the midst of a very confusing spiritual experience within a Buddhist temple in Rangoon, we found humanity and a friend. Our hearts were warmed.

Later that day, our government-assigned tour guide took us to a lake in the middle of the city, away from all the listening ears. As we walked around the lake, she poured out her compassion for her country and her commitment to the incarcerated leader, Aung San Suu Kyi. For this recent college graduate and newly married young woman and government employee, it was a soul-searching discussion. As we were leaving the country the next day, she instructed the driver to go a different way to the airport. The government driver looked disgusted. We drove through the city as she told us that within the next block we would see a fence of a certain color. On the corner would be a sign indicating the site was a school. In reality, she confided, it was the place where her "hope" was living under house arrest. This young woman's commitment to her country and her people served to deepen our faith in God who cares for all creation.

Both of us are interested in and committed to the scholarship that comes from the Jesus Seminar. Its process and published works aid our own faith development as we ask questions of, and make new connections with, the culture at the time of Jesus. We live in a society where so many attempt to convince others there is only "one way" or that one's personal proof of value is dependent upon the money one makes. Our own academic work and delightful encounters with persons from various cultures teach us to cherish spirituality as a continual adventure. So we read and delight in the color-coded Jesus sayings, as we attempt to meet *Jesus Again for the First Time*. Who was this man who grew up in a culture that expected one of their number would be the Messiah? All these less than mainstream ideas are part of our conversations as we travel in the car, sit at separate computers in the upstairs study, observe others in a restaurant, walk through the zoo with our grandchildren, or struggle with the appropriate language for a particular piece of writing.

As we travel in life, we enjoy religious background available in nontraditional ways. The character *Fidelma,* from the novels of Peter Tremayne, travels with us. Ellis Peter's *Brother Cadfael* is a necessary companion on many of our journeys. Through them, our souls are touched and broadened as we try to understand the pre-Christian religious history of an area, or the pre-Roman Christian history of Ireland and Scotland. Laurie King's *Mary Russell* traveled with us to Jerusalem. C. S. Song, Anna Deavere Smith, Karen Armstrong, Thich Nhat Hanh, and Ben Shawn, in print form, are constant companions.

Several years ago, we spent a few days in a typical tourist resort on the Amazon after attending a denominational event in Brazil. We had chosen the "resort" (we do not normally visit resorts) because it was new, not yet popular, and very inexpensive. One of the staff responsible for providing water transportation and clearing tables after meals was a young native of the area. We spent a morning with him and others from the site on a walking tour. We asked lots of questions. Several days later he asked if just the two of us would consider going with him in his canoe. We quickly agreed. As the day ended, he piloted us in a two-person canoe through the heavy undergrowth of the rain forest, pointing out plants used for particular medical cures, helping us hear the parrots flying far above the tops of the dense trees, warning us of the snakes in the water. The three of us were in the canoe as the water gently lapped the top on both sides. DarEll needed to sit completely still, or we would capsize. Diane needed to trust our guide. Further and further into the rain forest we traveled until we were not capable of distinguishing the sky from the earth. The reflections were such that, whether we were looking up or looking down, it appeared as though we could see a very long way. In every direction we saw the same combination of reflected earth, growth, water, and sky. In this symmetrically reflective universe we were three very small points within all of the evident life. The three of us, from two very different cultures and religious traditions, knew what it was like to be embraced by the Creator. Our guide in the spiritual adventure was one who spoke very little English, yet willingly shared his greatest treasure. He piloted us safely back to the dock just as the sun set.

We live in a different house than we did sixteen years ago. The African masks, now supplemented with those from other adventures, continue to hang on the wall at the entrance of our current home. They are reminders that the African experience was important to DarEll who was raised in very conservative evangelical North Dakota. Our own perceptions are so limited and can easily be enriched by the views of others. DarEll remembers working with his students as they wrote African stories to illustrate the meaning of some of Jesus' parables. "I do not think what you have written makes the same point," he would tell his students. They assured him that if Jesus had told the parables in Africa, this is the way he would have told them. Yes, the writings of the students did have the same meaning, but DarEll's spirituality had to be enlarged to see it.

So we continue to question, to experience, and to discuss.

16

Marriage As a Spiritual Path

Harville Hendrix and Helen Hunt

The person who desires to see the Living God face to face must not seek God in the empty firmament of the mind, but in human love.

Twenty-four years ago we initiated our relationship with a passionate discussion of this sentence. We spent a good hour on our first date going back and forth about what Dostoevsky really meant when he wrote these words in *The Brothers Karamazov*. What does he mean by "the Living God"? Why *can't* we find God in the mind, but only in human love? Human love is fractious and inconstant, as well as redeeming and healing. So, what *is* he saying about God and what *is* he saying about love.

We should have known this was an auspicious beginning. During three years of intense friendship, we turned our initial attraction into a lifelong commitment. There was no way for us to know, however, that we would spend the next twenty-three years trying to understand what it meant to find God, not in the mind, but in human love. Maybe it's no accident that Dostoevsky himself wrote these words at the end of his life, after he had experienced years of suffering and loss, as well as love. What a long, intense and awe-struck journey it has been for us, too, to find our way back to his pearl of wisdom.

All we knew that first night was that we loved to discuss, debate, and push the boundaries of our own understanding. We both had children from previous marriages, we both came from Southern Baptist upbringings, and we both loved to engage in the kind of academic thinking and writing that our educational backgrounds had prepared us for.

We had no trouble listing the reasons that our match would be a good one. Admittedly, we had friends who approached us gingerly with certain worried questions. Did we realize that there was a thirteen-year age difference? Did we think it would matter that Helen was from a wealthy and socially prominent Dallas family, while Harville was the son of Georgia sharecroppers? Had we considered how we would combine Emily Dickinson's poetry with Star Trek or classical music with down-home country? We politely acknowledged these differences, but we were not worried. We were confident that our psychology and counseling backgrounds would help us find the sacred middle ground where we could meet.

Beyond the cognitive reasoning that went into our decision to marry was the blissful narcotic of love. We treasured each other's company. We found ourselves daydreaming about the dynamic personal and professional partnership we would form. We would make up for our past mistakes. We would heal each other's wounds. We would be wonderful parents for our blended family and for the children we would have together. We would have the best marriage there ever was.

In other words, we were like any other couple in the first stage of romantic love. And it was wonderful. We had two more children and found ourselves very busy with six children, responsibilities for the family business, large extended families, and demanding careers.

By the time we got to the second stage of our relationship—the power struggle—an interesting thing had happened. Our personal fascination with the subject of relationships had become a major focus for our professional careers. We had incorporated our interest in feminism into a working theory of marriage as partnership. It turned out that this private and ongoing investigation into the dynamics of couple relationships would grow to be an international movement.

With the publication in 1991 of *Getting the Love You Want: A Guide for Couples*, a nation of troubled marriages was introduced to Imago Relationship Therapy. People were now looking to us for help in understanding why their marriages were rocky and what they could do to make them better. Thousands of people let us know that they were finding help through the books, workshops, and public appearances we offered. The Imago Institute began to train therapists all over the world. We had succeeded in coalescing our years of thinking about the potential of romantic partnership into an exciting and demanding *professional* partnership. We had become relationship experts.

Throughout the work of building Imago, we kept in touch with our spiritual values. Our Christian faith has always been a quiet river running under and through every other part of our lives. But, increasingly, we kept it compartmentalized. More and more we spoke and thought in the language of the existentialist, the pragmatist, the rationalist, and the humanist. We knew the Bible stories and went to church as a family, but we lost the habit of approaching life from a Jesus perspective. We had sought enlightenment through the mind and had been rewarded for it. We were in danger of believing that that was precisely where the Living God could be found.

Our marriage was progressing through the normal evolution of all relationships, and we began to exemplify the power struggle that we had so eloquently written about. Our knowledge did not seem to help us stop sparring. We disagreed and were disagreeable. We were disappointed. We were distanced. We wondered how we could have made this mistake, *again*, for the second time. Evidently, growing a successful theory of marriage had taken time and energy away from growing a successful marriage.

Four years ago, we were on the point of divorce. Not our own expertise, nor our own six books, nor anyone else's seemed able to help us. There was nothing wrong with our work or our ideas. We knew we had saved many relationships with our theory of "conscious marriage." But we had kept our insights and our ideas in our heads and not allowed them to penetrate deeper into our souls. To put it simply, we could not use what we knew because we had intellectualized the material instead of integrating it.

We decided to divorce. We went to the Imago community with our decision, and they accepted it with shock and sadness, pledging their support and prayers. That was a moment of truth for us. Seeing our separation through their eyes was a wake-up call. The possibility of our failure suddenly became very real. We agreed to delay the divorce for one year while we tried to dig deeper into what we knew and find a way to repair our relationship.

For us this meant reconnecting with the spiritual dimension of our lives, experiencing once again the Living God working through us. Not so much *reading about* these matters as *living in* their power. We were hungry to rediscover what it meant to be the children of God, following marriage as a sacred path. We opened ourselves to the possibility that faith could heal our broken relationship. As we look back, there are three ways this transformation happened in our lives.

1. What would God want us to do?

One day, after we had locked horns yet again, we remembered something a friend had shared with us. She credited her solid marriage to a question she and her husband asked themselves when they faced conflict. We stopped our argument and awkwardly asked ourselves: *What would God want us to do?* Even though it was unfamiliar territory, this simple question pulled us out of our conflict and into reflection. There was a subtle shift from acrimony to acceptance as we became conscious of a larger perspective that included things like loving one's enemy, forgiving trespasses, gratitude for one's gifts, and the sense of being loved even in our broken state.

We continued to use this question as a return call to the spiritual dimension of our relationship, and our answer became increasingly clear: *God would want us to love each other, as God loves us in every single interaction in our lives.* We had written about the potential of marriage to heal past wounds and bring out the best in people, but we had not had enough faith that it could happen for us. Were we like Moses, leading people to the promised land but fated never to see it ourselves? We realized we never would enter the promised land until we could see each other through God's love. When we began to turn to each other and look through that Divine light, the change was profound.

2. Be still, and know that I am God.

This sentence from Psalm 46:10 is simple, but its impact is palpable. There are many places in the Old and New Testaments where we are reminded of the sacred state of being silently receptive to the Spirit. Here is Luke 17:20-21:

> Once, having been asked by the Pharisees when the kingdom of God would come, Jesus replied, "The kingdom of God does not come with your careful observation, nor will people say, 'Here it is,' or 'There it is,' because the kingdom of God is within you." (NIV)

This sounds very much like our favorite quote from Dostoevsky. Our openness to spiritual direction was leading us to quiet our minds and look within ourselves and each other instead of always seeking answers from the outside.

As we worked our way back to a good marriage, we began to link scripture to Intentional Dialogue, which is the central process of Imago Relationship Therapy. The three steps in dialogue—mirroring, validation, and empathy—require both partners to slow down, listen carefully to each other, and honor what they hear. Each must heed the advice in James 1:19: "Be quick to hear, slow to speak, slow to anger" (RSV).

Although we have written about Intentional Dialogue in a secular way, we could now see the way in which it was holy. If God is best found in human love, then coming together in authentic partnership is a holy process. It is a path by which one could come to know the beloved and through the beloved, could come to know God. This careful listening became a kind of meditation for us, a stilling of the mind and heart, which allowed the presence of the other to enter. We learned to abandon the ego in order to leave room for a higher state of consciousness. Our relationship was becoming a spiritual path, and Intentional Dialogue was the daily practice.

We spent more time reading our Bible together, and everything we read seemed to point toward right relationship as a central part of being Christian. We began to understand that a good marriage is a sacrament, a mystery in which two people become conductors of agape love: the love of God, the kind of love in which concern for the welfare of the other is equal to, if not greater than, concern for the self. Martin Buber described this as a covenant relationship in which two people expand beyond their egos to make the safety and welfare of the other their primary concern. When this happens, God is present between the I and the Thou: "Love is responsibility of an I for a Thou" (Martin Buber, *I and Thou*, 2nd ed. [New York: Charles Scribner's Sons, 1958], 15).

3. To know with the heart as well as the mind

We gave ourselves twelve months to reconstruct our marriage on a new foundation. Every month that passed brought new insights and a deepening experience of marriage as a sacred path. Sometimes, we would look back at the way things were "before," and we could feel that we were changing.

There was the sense, for example, that each of us was entering into the other's experience with more willingness to participate in the reality of the other. We were able to let go of our own stubborn, rigid perceptions and see the world through each other's eyes. We were not able to put this change into words until we came across a remarkable book called *Women's Ways of Knowing* (Mary Field Belenky, Blythe Clinchy, Nancy Goldberger, and Jill Tarule, *Women's Ways of Knowing: The Development of Self, Voice, and Mind* [New York: Basic Books, 1986], 100-21). In it, the authors distinguish between separate and connecting knowing. As soon as we read about these two different ways of perceiving, we knew that it described the shift we were experiencing in our own lives.

Separate knowing is the process of accumulating the knowledge that forms the basis of science, philosophy, and psychology. Without separate knowing, for example, we would not have been able to develop Imago. When one is involved in the process of separate knowing, one moves away from the thing to be known in order to evaluate it. The goal is to be as objective as possible. One applies critical skills and asks such questions as: "What evidence supports this conclusion?" and "What are the problems with this theory?"

It is not hard to see how this kind of approach to intimate relationships leads to misunderstandings and resentments. Almost never do you want your partner to be your critic. Most often, close relationships thrive when there is a healthy dose of connected knowing. Connected knowing is when the knower moves *into* the thing to be known and tries it on. Judgment is suspended for a "deliberate, imaginative extension of . . . understanding into positions that initially feel wrong or remote. Connected knowing involves feeling because it is rooted in relationship, but it also involves thought" (Belenky et al., *Women's Ways*, 121). Martin Buber describes this kind of relational state as "a swing into the life of the other" in order to make the other real or present (Martin Buber, quoted in Nancy Goldberger, Blythe Clinchy, Mary Belenky, and Jill Mattuck Tarule, *Knowledge, Difference and Power: Essays Inspired by* Women's Ways of Knowing [New York: Basic Books, 1996], 217).

We could see that our academic training and our professional success had led us to try to solve our personal problems by using the techniques of separate knowing. Gradually, we came to see that we needed to get close enough to "try on" each other's experiences. When we were able to enter into each other's lives, the foundation of our new marriage was built on connection instead of separation.

During the year we had pledged to rebuild our marriage, we worked to bring all three of our spiritual insights into play. When our direction was unclear, we asked what God would want us to do. We manifested Divine love between us by listening carefully to each other through Intentional Dialogue. As we listened with the "generous thinking" of connected knowing, we experienced the profound change from communication to communion.

At the end of our year's journey, the marriage we had dreamed about was within our grasp. On January 1, 2000, as the new millennium began, we stood before God, family, and friends at Riverside Church in New York City in a blinding snowstorm and recommitted ourselves to each other and to our marriage. We walked together into that promised land along the spiritual path that God had given us. For that path, we are deeply grateful. It has allowed us to see the Living God in each other's face and to know without any doubt that what we are seeing is the reflection of Divine love.

Recommended Readings on Marriage

Gottman, John Mordechai, and Nan Silver. *The Seven Principles for Making Marriage Work.* New York: Crown Publishing Group, 1999.

Hendrix, Harville. *Getting the Love You Want: A Guide for Couples.* New York: H. Holt and Co., 2001.

Hunt, Richard A., and Joan A. Hunt. *Growing Love in Christian Marriage.* Nashville: Abingdon Press, 2001.

Jordan, Pamela L., Scott M. Stanley, and Howard J. Markman. *Becoming Parents: How to Strengthen Your Marriage as Your Family Grows.* San Francisco: Jossey-Bass Publishers, 1999.

Markman, Howard J., Susan L. Blumberg, and Scott M. Stanley. *Fighting for Your Marriage: Positive Steps for Preventing Divorce and Preserving a Lasting Love.* San Francisco: Jossey-Bass Publishers, 2001.

Pipher, Mary Bray. *The Shelter of Each Other: Rebuilding Our Families.* New York: G. P. Putnam's Sons, 1996.

Wallerstein, Judith S., and Sandra Blakeslee. *The Good Marriage: How and Why Love Lasts.* Boston: Houghton Mifflin, 1995.

Walsh, Froma. *Strengthening Family Resilience.* New York: Guilford Press, 1998.

Whitehead, Evelyn Eaton, and James D. Whitehead. *Marrying Well: Stages on the Journey of Christian Marriage.* Garden City, N.J.: Image Books, 1983.

Contributors

Esther Kwon and Clifford Iwao Arinaga have lived in Honolulu, Hawaii, during most of their forty-six years of marriage. Proving the adage that lawyers never really retire, they remain active as volunteers in several public interest law organizations and community projects. Their three grown children, Susan, Bruce, and Paul, and their seven grandchildren provide unending joy as well as vociferous opinions at lively family reunions. The Arinagas are members of Wesley United Methodist Church in East Honolulu, where they have found a loving and nurturing congregation and a pastor who has deepened their understanding of the language of faith.

Cynthia and John Astle of Dallas celebrated "twenty-five glorious years of marriage" in 2001. The marriage of these high school sweethearts has produced a son, Sean Damon, who graduated from high school in 2001. John is manager of electronic prepress for a printing firm and has led seminars on digital publishing for church communicators. He is currently writing a trade book on digital publishing. Cynthia is editor of the *United Methodist Reporter* national weekly newspaper and has published two books, *Faithfully Yours* (Dallas: UMR Communications, 1996) and *Believing Is Seeing* (coauthored with W. Ginger Everitt [Hawaii: Spin Productions, 1999]). The Astles are active members of Casa View United Methodist Church in Dallas, where John sings in the choir, Cynthia is a lay preacher, and both frequently teach Sunday school classes for various age levels. They are beginning to contemplate a happy retirement, traveling around America in a recreational vehicle, seeking the perfect place to settle down and grow old together.

Joseph Cunneen was studying in Paris on the GI Bill in 1948 when told by activists in the JEC (student Christian movement) to look up **Sally** McDevitt, a young woman in New York who was writing a book about love. He followed their advice, and their fifty-two years of marriage brought him a life partner who was to share in the founding of the international ecumenical quarterly *Cross Currents*. Joe taught theater, comparative literature, and religion at Fordham, the College of New Rochelle, Baruch, and Mercy College, interrupted by thirteen years as Senior Editor at Holt. Since 1988, he has been movie critic for *National Catholic Reporter*. He is now working on a book about

Robert Bresson. Sally Cunneen is professor emeritus of English at Rockland Community College and the author of four books: *Sex: Female, Religion: Catholic* (New York: Holt, Rinehardt, and Winston, 1968); *Mother Church: What the Experience of Women Is Teaching Her* (New York: Paulist Press, 1991); *Contemporary Meditations on the Everyday God* (Chicago: Thomas More Press, 1976); and most recently *In Search of Mary: The Woman and the Symbol* (New York: Ballantine Books, 1996), which was chosen as Book of the Year by the College Theology Society.

Ulrike and Clifton F. Guthrie have been married since 1988, and both are Episcopalians. Ulrike has been an editor of academic books on religion for fifteen years, first in her native England with Cambridge University Press, then in the U.S. with Abingdon Press. Her master's degree is in German and from St. Andrew's University, Scotland. Clifton is Assistant Professor of Homiletics and Pastoral Studies at Bangor Theological Seminary. He earned his Ph.D. in theological studies at Emory University, where he also taught as an adjunct professor. Clifton is co-editor of *Doxology: A Journal of Worship*, editor of *For All the Saints* (Akron, Ohio: Order of Saint Luke Publications, 1995), and author of *Faith: Living a Spiritual Life* (Nashville: Abingdon Press, 2000). Ulrike and Clifton's recent move to Maine enables her to stay at home in their rambling old house in Bangor to look after their children, Thomas and Emelia, and to work as a freelance editor and translator.

James A. and Marsha Harnish share their life together in Tampa, where Jim is the Senior Pastor at Hyde Park United Methodist Church. He is a 1972 graduate of Asbury Theological Seminary and has served three other congregations in Florida. Jim's books include *Journey to the Center of the Faith: An Explorer's Guide to Christian Living* (Nashville: Abingdon Press, 2001); and *Passion, Power, and Praise: A Model for Men's Spirituality from the Life of David* (Nashville: Abingdon Press, 2000). Marsha is an elementary school educator who taught in public schools for twenty years and presently directs a tutoring ministry for underprivileged children. They have two daughters and one son-in-law.

Harville Hendrix and Helen Hunt are cofounders of the Institute for Imago Relationship Therapy, with its international office in Orlando, Florida, and they are collaborators in the creation of Imago Relationship Therapy and the concepts of "conscious marriage" and "conscious parenting." Their personal and intellectual partnership led to the publication of the three bestsellers, including *Getting the Love You Want: A Guide for Couples* (New York: H. Holt & Co., 2001) and *Keeping the Love You Find: A Guide for Singles* (New York: Pocket Books, 1992) authored by Hendrix. He and Hunt are coauthors of *The Couples Companion: Meditations and Exercises for Getting the Love You Want* (New York: Pocket Books, 1994), *The Personal Companion: Meditations and Exercises for Keeping the Love You Find* (New York: Pocket Books, 1995), *Giving the Love That Heals: A Guide for Parents* (New York: Pocket Books, 1997), and *The Parenting Companion: Meditations and Exercises for Giving the Love That Heals* (New York: Pocket Books, 1999).

Joan and Richard Hunt were married in 1951 and have two sons—Randy and his wife, Annetta, have two children, and Ron and his wife, Sarah, have three children. Richard and Joan coauthored two books for Abingdon Press, *Caring Couples Network: Handbook* (Nashville: Discipleship Resources, 1996) and *Growing Love in Christian Marriage* (Nashville: Abingdon Press, 2001), the official marriage manual of The United Methodist Church. Since 1985, Richard has been professor of psychology at Fuller Seminary Graduate School of Psychology in Pasadena, California, after holding the same position at Southern Methodist University for twenty years. He is an ordained United Methodist minister, licensed psychologist, and Diplomat with the American Board of Professional Psychology, and holds degrees from Texas Wesleyan University, Perkins School of Theology, and Texas Christian University. For thirteen years, they served pastorates in Texas. Joan earned her degree in speech pathology from Southern Methodist University.

Kathleen DeSutter Jordan is a registered nurse. She graduated from Webster University and has an M.S. in nursing from Pace University. She has worked primarily with those who are physically and mentally handicapped. **Patrick Jordan** did postgraduate work at the Graduate Theological Union in Berkeley. He is the managing editor of *Commonweal* and coedited *Commonweal Confronts the Century: Liberal Convictions, Catholic Traditions* (New York: Simon & Schuster, 1999). They have two adult children.

Diane Kenney and DarEll T. Weist celebrated sixteen years of marriage in 2001. Diane, ordained in the Christian Church (Disciples of

Christ), has served in ecumenical campus ministry for thirty years. She began at Stanford University, moved to Mills College, relocated to Youngstown State University in Ohio, and now ministers at the University of Southern California. (They met when he was on the search committee that hired her.) DarEll, who was ordained as a United Methodist forty years ago, has been a pastor, theological teacher in Africa, church bureaucrat, and foundation president. Out of her ecumenical campus ministry, Diane created a social service agency that involves students (for credit) providing genuine help to the urban homeless. DarEll, as developer, has built 141 units of affordable housing to help create a community for First UMC, Los Angeles. As President and CEO of the Los Angeles United Methodist Urban Foundation, he is involved in "faith-based" development throughout Southern California.

Bonnie J. and Donald E. Messer live in Denver. Bonnie is a licensed psychology in private practice and holds a Ph.D. in counseling psychology from the University of Denver and an M.S.W. from Boston University. Don, an ordained United Methodist minister, serves as Henry White Warren Professor of Practical Theology and President Emeritus of The Iliff School of Theology. He is author of nine books, including *Contemporary Images of Christian Ministry* (Nashville: Abingdon Press, 1989), *Christian Ethics and Political Action* (Valley Forge: Judson Press, 1984), *How Shall We Die? Helping Christians Debate Assisted Suicide* (Nashville: Abingdon Press, 1997), and *Calling Church and Seminary into the 21st Century* (Nashville: Abingdon Press, 1995).

June and James W. Moore of Houston celebrated their forty-second wedding anniversary in 2001. They both grew up in Memphis and have served churches in Tennessee, Ohio, Louisiana, and Texas. June attended Lambuth University and received her B.A. from Otterbein College. Jim received a B.A. from Lambuth University and M.Div. from the Methodist Theological School in Ohio. He was awarded a Doctor of Divinity from Centenary College. The Moores have served St. Luke's United Methodist Church in Houston since 1984. During that time, Jim has been a best-selling author and has written more than twenty books, including *When Grief Breaks Your Heart* (Nashville: Abingdon Press, 1994), *When All Else Fails . . . Read the Instructions* (Nashville: Dimensions for Living, 1993), and *Yes, Lord, I Have Sinned, But I Have Several Excellent Excuses* (Nashville: Abingdon Press, 1991), and *9/11—What a Difference a Day Makes*

(Nashville: Dimensions for Living, 2002). The Moores have two married children, Jodi (husband Danny) and Jeff (wife Claire), and their hobby is celebrating their four grandchildren: Sarah, Paul, Dawson, and Daniel.

William A. and Kristine Ritter celebrated their thirty-fifth wedding anniversary in 2001. Both are Detroit area natives and lifelong United Methodists. Kris's academic background includes attending Michigan State and Wayne State universities, while Bill's includes attending Albion College and Yale University. For the last thirty-seven years, Bill has served United Methodist congregations in the Detroit Annual Conference. Currently, he is in his ninth year as the senior minister of First United Methodist Church, Birmingham, Michigan. For the last decade, Kris has been a self-employed training consultant whose primary client has been the Ford Motor Company. They have one daughter, Julie, who is currently enrolled in an MBA program at Harvard.

Robert and Esther Schnase and their sons, Karl and Paul, live in McAllen, Texas. Robert is a pastor and writer. He has published numerous articles on Christian vocation and clergy support systems, as well as two books: *Ambition in Ministry: Our Spiritual Struggle with Success, Achievement, and Competition* (Nashville: Abingdon Press, 1993), and *Testing and Reclaiming Your Call to Ministry* (Nashville: Abingdon Press, 1991). He serves on the board of directors of several statewide and national denominational agencies, and he chairs the Order of Elders of the Southwest Texas Conference. Robert enjoys studying Spanish, traveling in Latin America, and running marathons. Esther teaches high school English. She's an avid reader and enjoys singing for the church and supporting their sons in their school, church, and scouting activities. Esther and Robert have been married for twenty-one years.

Don and Jean Shelby recently celebrated their forty-second wedding anniversary. They served three United Methodist congregations in Southern California during Don's forty-five years in the active ministry: St. Matthews in Hacienda Heights, St. Marks in San Diego, and, for twenty-three years, First Church in Santa Monica. Jean retired in 1997 from a career in early childhood education, and Don retired from the California-Pacific Annual Conference in 1998. They now reside in the Los Osos-Morro Bay area along California's central coast, midway between their two married daughters, Dana Knowles and Darla

Dyson, their sons-in-law, Mike and Eric, and their five lively grand-children, Shelby, John, Matthew, Ruby, and Olivia. Don grew up in Kansas where he graduated from Baker University and then Claremont School of Theology in California. Jean is a native of Ohio and graduated from Ohio State University. Don is author of *Unsettling Season* (Nashville: Upper Room Books, 1989), *Bold Expectations of the Gospel* (Nashville: Upper Room Books, 1983), *Forever Beginning: Exploration of the Faith for New Believers* (Nashville: Upper Room Books, 1987), and *Meeting the Messiah* (Nashville: Upper Room Books, 1980).

Karen M. and Howard W. Stone were married in 1963. Their one child, Christine, lives in Italy, is married to William Po, and has two daughters, Elizabeth and Caitlin. Karen was born in Minneapolis and received her B.F.A. and M.F.A. degrees from Arizona State University. She has taught art at all levels, from elementary school to university, and presently is an art specialist for the Fort Worth Independent School District. She has exhibited her work in museums and galleries throughout the U.S. and is included in a number of collections worldwide. Her book *Image and Spirit: Finding Meaning in Visual Art* will be published by Augsburg Books in 2003. Howard was also born in Minneapolis and received his B.A. from Augsburg College, M.Div. from Lutheran Theological Seminary at Philadelphia, and Ph.D. from the School of Theology at Claremont. He is an ordained Lutheran minister, pastoral counselor, and psychologist. Since 1979, Howard has been Professor of Pastoral Theology and Pastoral Counseling at Brite Divinity School, Texas Christian University. He has published a dozen books, among them *Brief Pastoral Counseling* (Minneapolis: Fortress Press, 1994); *Crisis Counseling* (Minneapolis: Fortress Press, 1993); *Theological Context for Pastoral Care Giving: Word in Deed* (New York: Haworth Pastoral Press, 1996); *Depression and Hope: New Insights for Pastoral Counseling* (Minneapolis: Fortress Press, 1998); and *Strategies for Brief Pastoral Counseling* (Minneapolis: Fortress Press, 2001).

John and Carolyn A. Twiname have been married for forty-seven years and have three grown daughters. For ten years, they served together as copresidents of The HealthCare Chaplaincy, a multifaith center that provides skilled spiritual support and clinical pastoral education in partnership with nearly thirty medical facilities in the greater New York City area. Prior to that, Carolyn held various management positions in the nonprofit and public sectors. John has worked for private businesses, the federal government, and nonprofit organizations in various health-related fields. In addition to having a B.A. in economics from Cornell and an M.B.A. from Harvard, John is ordained by the Presbyterian Church (USA). Carolyn earned her B.S. in education from Northwestern University and her Master of Government and Public Administration from American University.

Reflections on Marriage and Spiritual Growth

Study Guide

John D. Schroeder

Marriage is the ultimate spiritual journey, according to Joseph Campbell as interviewed by Bill Moyers in *The Power of Myth*. This book offers sixteen reflections on this journey from Christian couples who share their insights through essays on their marriage experiences. If you are discussing this book with others, this guide offers questions for each of the sixteen chapters for you to use.

Customize your discussions by using as many questions as you desire based upon your available time and how many chapters you cover during each session. For example, if the sixteen chapters are being covered in four sessions, you may want to select one or two questions from every four chapters. An eight-week study would cover two chapters during each session.

Participants can select the questions they would like to discuss, or the group leader can pick questions that he or she feels would result in a good discussion. The leader and participants can also create their own discussion questions from the material.

It may take you from forty-five minutes to an hour for each session. Plan for the final ten minutes to be spent in individual introspection on the reflection question. Paper and pencils will be needed. A short final prayer to conclude the session is printed at the end of each lesson.

1. A Love for All Time

1. How does 1 Corinthians 13:4-8*a* reflect the central role that the Christian faith has played in your partnership? Has this passage given you strength and guidance for your marriage? Why do you think this passage is often used in a marriage ceremony? What reminders and hope does it represent?

2. What have you learned about love from your partner? In what ways has your partner been a teacher or an example? Discuss an incident from your marriage that was a learning event. At what point did you realize that marriage is a spiritual journey?

3. How has your love changed over the years? Discuss a weakness that has become stronger. What has been a strength for both of you? What has been a weakness in your marriage? What do you think has caused your love to change? Explain.

4. Take the roles of Cynthia and John. Select a single trait of love that is given in this passage, such as love is patient or love is kind, and take a few moments to verbally express what the trait means to each of you based upon your marriage experience. Share an example based upon an incident during your marriage.

5. Can you strongly identify with one of the observations made by Cynthia or John? Was there a remark that one of them made that really hit home or had a major impact on you? Select one of their observations and discuss how it relates to love, your marriage, and the journey of marriage.

Reflection Question

6. Do your own personal evaluation based on the passage 1 Corinthians 13:4-8*a*. Take each of the ten components, from love is patient through love never dies, and write down some thoughts about love as you have experienced it through your marriage. Reflect on your strengths and weaknesses. Consider how the love of Christ has been an anchor in your marriage. Discuss your observations with each other.

Closing Prayer

Dear God, we thank you for giving us the perfect example of love in your son, Jesus. Help us demonstrate our love to each other and to others each day of our lives. Grant that we may be honest with each other, recognizing our faults. May we use the power of prayer to meet the challenges we face and to continually strengthen our relationship. Help us grow in love toward you and toward each other. Amen.

2. Married Couples Make the Best Peaceful Wrecks

1. Consider how marriage is a learning experience. Discuss the following statements: "Marriage has taught me a great deal about what it means to be human" and "Marriage has taught me a great deal about my own limitations." Share how you had to learn about your partner's needs, preferences, and annoyances. What are some of the things you have learned through marriage?

2. Joseph Cunneen says that he grew up believing that all married couples were happy and that his view of marriage was partially based on the portrayals of married couples in the movies. Recall your perception of marriage before you got married. Discuss some of the myths of marriage and the unexpected aspects of becoming husband and wife. In what ways were you ignorant? Do you think couples about to be married are less ignorant today?

3. This essay discusses how births and deaths change a marriage. The authors say, "Christian marriage implies an openness to the gift of life." Share your thoughts about how children and death have been a part of your spiritual development. As you have shared together how life begins and ends, how

has it brought you closer together? How do children affect a marriage? How have you dealt with the death of parents or loved ones?

4. Discuss the meaning behind the title, "Married Couples Make the Best Peaceful Wrecks," as revealed in the last paragraph. Do you agree with this observation? What are some of the blessings of a long marriage?

5. A good marriage needs a broad network of support, according to the authors. While a husband and wife need to become best friends, what else is needed to make a marriage work? How does having a broad circle of friends enhance the marriage relationship? Share how your friends have helped your marriage.

Reflection Question

6. "To live up to the impossible promise of Christian marriage (For better, for worse") requires God's help," according to the authors. Reflect on how God has been an active partner in your marriage and how your marriage has been blessed and strengthened by God. Where have you seen God's hand in your relationship? List some of the gifts and blessings given to you by God.

Closing Prayer

Dear God, we thank you for this time together to discuss the blessings of marriage. We are grateful for the insights we have gained from discussing this chapter and our marriage experiences. Help us be open to you and to each other. May we continue to grow together in Christian love. Amen.

3. Tied to Be Fit

1. William Ritter's observations of the "ever-changing nuptial parade" reveal how the institution of marriage has evolved. He notes how his homilies have changed from stern and sober warnings to encouraging words. Try to contrast and compare how you see marriage has changed over the years. Why is holding a marriage together more difficult? Is anything about marriage easier now? What challenges do today's couples face that you did not face?

2. Read Ecclesiastes 4:9-12 and discuss what the text means to you. How does the message apply to marriage? Where does the title of this essay, "Tied to Be Fit," come in? Do you agree with the author? Explain.

3. The author gives four reasons that "two are better than one." List each of the four reasons and relate to each reason with an example from your marriage. Can you think of any other reasons? What are some advantages of being a "one"? Why shouldn't everyone be a "two"?

4. Do you agree with the author that the "third strand" is God? Explain. What is his rationale that God needs to be a factor? How has this been evident in your marriage? What is a marriage like that is missing the "third strand"? What are some symptoms of a marriage that is missing God?

5. In the epilogue, Kristine Ritter points out that in the past, two were essential for survival. She adds that today, both men and women have more choices. What are some of the choices? Are choices a good or bad thing? Explain. What are some of the choices that you made that had a major impact, for good or bad, on your marriage?

Reflection Question

6. In the movie *It's a Wonderful Life*, the hero experiences what life would have been like if he had never been born. Imagine your life if you had never found your spouse and become married. Reflect on what this reality would be like. What would you have missed? What would others have missed? How many lives have been touched by your marriage?

Closing Prayer

Dear God, we thank you for the gift of marriage. We remember the joy and the struggles and how your love has sustained us. Please continue to bless, and be the foundation of, our marriage. May we continue to look to you in the good and bad times. And help us always remember your goodness. Amen.

4. Water into Wine

1. "There's no place I'd rather be than here, and no people I'd rather be with than the people in this room." At which, if any, points in your marriage could you say this statement with assurance? How often is a couple at a resting place of satisfaction in their marriage? Why do most couples constantly look ahead, wanting to move on and move up?

2. According to the authors, Ron and Lyla Schnase lived ordinary lives and lived them together for fifty years. How common is this? Is this something to aspire to? From this essay, what contributed to their long marriage? Other marriages may have high drama, overcome great obstacles, or be full of passion or conflict. For you, what is an ideal marriage? What's the difference between ordinary and extraordinary?

3. The authors of this essay detail the stages of a marriage, from young love, to a period of figuring things out, followed by a maturing and discovering period. Consider the stages of your marriage. Try to list and define them. How has your love grown and changed over the years? Do all marriages go through the same stages? What are the easiest and most difficult stages?

4. The authors observe, "Some marriages adapt; some break apart. Almost all experience fraying at the edges." What is necessary in order for a married couple to be able to adapt and cope with fraying at the edges? What part does love play? Is faith a factor? Does luck or chance play a part? What is the difference between adapting and breaking apart?

5. Consider the enormous amount of faith that it takes to maintain a marriage. The author notes that newly married couples have no idea what their journey will require, where it will take them, the challenges it will

bring, or what resources will be needed. Certainly hope is needed to maintain a faith and a marriage. What else is needed? How has your faith been
tested, and what helped you maintain your faith?

Reflection Question

6. Look back at your marriage and spiritual journey, and reflect on your
expectations. First, think back to your wedding day and what you expected
from your marriage. How many expectations were realistic? What did you
expect from your spouse? Then, look at what you didn't expect. List some
of the surprises, both good and bad. Consider what helped you cope with
the expected and unexpected.

Closing Prayer

Dear God, we thank you for this opportunity to take another look at our lives,
our marriage, and your many blessings. We thank you for our partner and all
that we have shared together. Help us continue to grow together in faith and
in love. May Christ continue to be the center of our home. Be with us during
the coming week. Amen.

5. Marriage on the Road: An Adventure in Faith

1. In what ways do you relate to the journey of John and Carolyn Twiname?
In what ways has your journey been different? What impressed you while
reading their story? How were you challenged by what you read?

2. The authors each share the foundations of their faith in the beginning of
this essay. Take a few moments to share the foundations of your faith.
How did your parents influence your faith? How regularly did you attend
church? Was there a turning point where your faith became stronger?
When you got married, was your foundation of faith similar to that of your
spouse? Explain. How strong a foundation of faith is needed for couples
about to be married?

3. During their thirties, the authors discovered a key to deepening their relationship: "letting Christ be the 'head of our family'—and of our marriage."
Discuss this key and any other keys you have discovered during your marriage. What changes occur when Christ becomes the head of the family?
Does marriage become easier? If so, how?

4. In their fifties, the authors detail "an adventure in faith" where their
prayer was that God would provide a ministry opportunity for John. Think
back on your marriage and share an "adventure in faith" that you experienced where you trusted in God through prayer to open a door. How did
your adventure begin? Was it a turning point for anything? How did it
change your marriage?

5. The authors discuss many prayers that were answered during their marriage. What prayers did God answer for you? Were the prayers answered in

a way you expected? How did you deal with prayers where the answer was no? How did your prayer life strengthen your marriage?

Reflection Question

6. The authors give many examples of gratitude and believe that gratitude is a great gift to cultivate in a marriage. Couples are grateful both to God and to each other. Reflect on how a spirit of gratitude strengthens a marriage and how grateful you are to God and your spouse. Think about how your spirit of gratitude was cultivated, and list some specific examples from your marriage.

Closing Prayer

Dear God, we thank you for the adventure of faith that has been so important in our marriage. Thank you for being with us during our spiritual journey and for helping us along the way. Help us continue to grow together in faith toward you and in deeper love for each other. May we appreciate you more and all you have done for us. Amen.

6. Two for the Road: Lessons We Have Learned Along the Way

1. The authors compare their marriage to a road trip based on Genesis 12, when God says, "Go!" and Abram and Sarai get up and go. How has your marriage been like a road trip? Have you ever felt called by God to travel somewhere? Have there been any detours along the way? What have you learned during your travels?

2. Jim and Marsha Harnish believe that "faith means walking in obedience to the call of God with little or no clarity about exactly where the road will lead, but with absolute trust in the One who is leading the way. Faith is defined by the direction in which our feet are moving." How has your trust in God grown during your journey? Give some examples of how your faith has grown and changed over the years.

3. James Harnish has a ring engraved with the words of James 1:17: "Every good and perfect gift comes from God." Consider the gifts you have been given by God. What gifts did you each bring into your marriage? How have you benefited from the gifts you received from God and each other? How have these gifts been a blessing to others? What was your most recent blessing?

4. The value of Christian friendships is one of the lessons that James and Marsha Harnish have learned on their journey together. Recall some early Christian friendships that influenced your marriage. How did friendships with others help you build a healthy marriage? What lessons have you learned from other couples? How have your friendships changed over the years? Why?

5. The authors share how God has helped them hold on in the hard places. What are the hard places in a marriage? Have you shared health problems

or financial challenges? How has God helped you through death and disappointments? Think about past stresses in your relationship and share how you worked things out. And finally, what have you learned from the hard times you have shared?

Reflection Question

6. Marriage is hard work with many rewards, according to the authors. Take some time to reflect on the work that has gone into your marriage. Think about the discipline involved and how you learned to focus your time and energy. After considering the hard work, look back at the accomplishments and rewards that have come about through your efforts. Take time to count your blessings and give thanks for what you have been given and what has been accomplished.

Closing Prayer

Dear God, marriage is a journey with many bumps in the road and nice surprises along the way. Thank you for guiding us on our road trip. Thank you for your protection, direction, and patience. You have blessed us with many gifts. Thank you. May we continue to rely on you to be our guide during the rest of our journey. Amen.

7. Communicating in the Family: Things to Avoid Like the Plague

1. June and Jim Moore give several examples and consequences of good and bad communication. Think back on the past year and share one example of good communication with your spouse. Talk about the difference it made. Now, look back and discuss an example of poor communication and the resulting problem it caused. Give some elements of good communication and symptoms of bad communication.

2. This essay also alerts us to the danger of mind games and false expectations. We need to be able to tell our partner what we want, need, feel, think, and expect so he or she doesn't have to guess or wonder what is wrong. In your own words, give an example of a mind game. Discuss the causes of mind games and the damage they can cause.

3. The authors warn about dumping emotional garbage on the dinner table. They state that in the Christian home, every meal should be a kind of Holy Communion, a time of celebration, love, and thankfulness. Dinner is not a place to discuss emotional things. Consider some of the reasons why emotional garbage gets shared at the dinner table, and talk about how this practice can be avoided.

4. We need to be careful what we put into words. Words can cause sickness and destruction. But they can also help and heal. The choice is ours. Share a time when you were hurt by words. How did you feel? Were you able to forgive and forget, or did the words change you? On the flip side, recall

some words of appreciation and kindness that were spoken to you. How did these words make you feel about yourself and the person who spoke them? Did it change your day? Explain.

5. Explain the concept of "the first four minutes" as described by the authors. See how this feels by role-playing with your spouse. Pretend you have not seen each other for a week. Take four minutes each to offer encouragement and acceptance to each other. Later this week, make an effort to put this concept into practice again.

Reflection Question

6. Take some time to reflect on how well you communicate with your spouse. Consider strengths, and then consider the weaknesses. Think about how communication problems have affected your marriage. Has your communication improved over the years? If you could change one thing, what would it be? Pray about this issue.

Closing Prayer

Dear Lord, you are the Word of God. You are God's idea for us, God's plan for us, and God's truth for us. May we always remember that Jesus is our measuring stick for communicating. Help our words be words of life, love, and healing. May we always think before we speak. Bless our marriage and all our communication. Amen.

8. Loving, Honoring, and Cherishing

1. Core beliefs and values serve as a foundation for married life. One of these values is faith in God's grace and a desire to be part of an active faith community. What difficulties arise when couples share different faith convictions? How does being an active member of a church enhance a marriage? Was religion an issue when you got married? How was this issue handled?

2. The authors discuss the importance of loving and honoring each other. They note that *love* and *honor* are both action verbs. In your own words, explain what honoring and loving your spouse means to you. What are some practical examples of how a husband or wife can honor a spouse on a daily basis? What roles do compromise and forgiveness play in loving your spouse? Give some examples from your marriage.

3. Related to love and honor is the value of cherishing. Relationships rupture because couples can take each other for granted. It's easy to forget that marriage is a privilege. In your own words, explain what "cherishing" means to you. How is it related to, and different from, love and honor? Give some examples of how a spouse can be cherished.

4. Love does not have an expiration date. A strong marriage includes a commitment to protecting and nurturing the marriage relationship. How does a strong sense of commitment develop in a marriage? What are some practical ways that a couple can protect and nurture their relationship? Discuss the importance of shared experiences and how you find adequate time to be together.

5. The fifth dimension of the author's wedding prayer accented a strong affirmation of their compassion for others. Relationships can be enhanced when couples embrace a shared social commitment or concern for others. Why is this so important in a marriage? What are some of the benefits to a marriage from active compassion for others? What role does your Christian faith play in this?

Reflection Question

6. This chapter was based on a special marriage prayer penned by the authors. Spend some time reflecting on the core beliefs and values that you share as a married couple. Have these values and beliefs changed over the years? If you desire, create a list of your values and beliefs, then incorporate them into a prayer that could be read during your next wedding anniversary.

Closing Prayer

Dear God, you are the source of strength for our marriage and our love. Help us continue to love, honor, and cherish each other as we continue on our journey together. Thank you for the many answered prayers and giving us answers and direction. Continue to bless us and be with us in good times as well as in troubled times. Amen.

9. Lucky Thirteen: Ritual, Faith, Marriage

1. What rituals were part of your wedding? Why do you think rituals are important? What do they add? How have marriage rituals changed over the years? Would you do anything differently if you had to do it all over again?

2. Look at some rituals that are found in the Bible. List some Christian rituals that are connected with birthdays, marriages, and funerals. What rituals or ceremonies did Jesus participate in during his ministry?

3. Think back upon how you planned your wedding. What were the most important details to you at the time? What activities went according to your plans? What surprises took place? How was your Christian faith reflected in the ceremony? When you look back on your wedding, what special memories do you have? If you had to do it all over again, what, if anything, would you change? Explain.

4. The authors discuss marriages that succeed and those that end in divorce. From your perspective and experience, what are some keys to success? What did you learn along the way about keeping your love and your marriage alive?

5. What impressed or challenged you from reading the marriage story of Ulrike and Cliff Guthrie? How was your courtship and marriage like theirs? How was it different?

Reflection Question

6. Make a list of all the rituals that are part of your family life each year. Think about how they got started. Why are they important? What do they add? Did this essay give you any ideas for new rituals or ways to celebrate your love and life together?

Closing Prayer

Dear God, our lives contain many rituals that remind us of our past and bring us together. We celebrate our love for each other and for the many blessings we have been given. Thank you for being with us in our rituals as we remember and give thanks for your goodness. Continue to bless us and those we love. Amen.

10. Words Matter: Marriage and the Language of Faith

1. What does "Don't mess with marriage" mean to you? How do people and politicians mess with marriage today? What motivates people to try to change or improve the institution of marriage? What happens when you mess with marriage? How does it get changed from what God intended it to be?

2. One of the messages about marriage in this essay is that marriage is sacred and no one should destroy the sanctity of marriage. What does the Bible say about marriage being sacred? What are some threats today to the sanctity of marriage? Is this an intentional threat where someone or an organization actually wants to destroy marriage? Explain.

3. The authors offer their reflections on the spiritual journey of marriage. They note that the seeds for the spiritual journey are actually planted before marriage. What seeds were planted before you got married? Did you realize the importance of the spiritual journey before you were married? Explain. What were your intentions for a spiritual journey together at the time you were married? What happened to these intentions?

4. Discuss some of the spiritual milestones of your journey of faith. What is the importance of these milestones? What do they measure? Do all married couples have the same spiritual milestones? Explain. If you could show some "photo snapshots" of spiritual values that sustained your marriage, what would they be?

5. The authors note that anxiety, conflict, and despair are the fault lines of a marriage and that they appear without any warning. How has this been the case in your marriage? What are some of the tests of faith that you have experienced? Give an example of a test of faith and how you survived that test.

Reflection Question

6. Marriages, as well as the lives of individuals, have turning points. These
are times when you discover that your resources of faith are insufficient to
meet your needs. Think back on some of the turning points in your own
life and your marriage. Did you recognize these turning points at the time?
How did they come about? How did they change you? Are you prepared for
future turning points?

Closing Prayer

Dear God, we thank you for the milestones in our spiritual journey of faith.
Thank you for blessing our marriage and helping us get through the tough
times. Help us continue to rely on you for strength and direction in our marriage. May we turn to you to maintain strong spiritual values so that we keep
our faith in you. Amen.

11. Marriage and Worship

1. How ignorant were you of the difficulties of marriage when you became
engaged? What had you learned from observing the marriage of your parents? Did it help or hinder you? What was the reaction of family and
friends to your engagement? Give some examples of things you didn't
know at the time, but learned later.

2. The authors discuss how marriage, for them, got better with the years.
Why is this the case for some couples and not others? Has your marriage
become better with time? In what way? Give some examples. What do you
think causes the bumps in a marriage to smooth out? This article points
out how marriage is like a series of cycles. Explain and name some of the
cycles.

3. Karen and Howard Stone note that they are very, very different people and
that being different is an important factor in their marriage. When you
were first married, did you believe your spouse was very different or very
similar to you? Explain. Are you different or the same today? How have
both of you changed? Discuss the importance of appreciating each other's
differences and recognizing the positive resources that each spouse offers.

4. The Stones believe that over the years, their interests, tastes, and beliefs
are becoming increasingly close, if not identical. How have you grown
closer together? What do you think causes people to grow closer together?
Discuss the importance of playing together. Give some examples from
your marriage.

5. How has attending church together enhanced your marriage? What is it
about worshiping together that strengthens your marriage union? How
does worship assist in honoring differences? How does praying together at
church and at mealtime bring you closer? Give some examples of how
mutual worship and prayer have been a blessing in your marriage.

Reflection Question

6. Consider how individual acts of worship—the prayers, bread, wine, liturgy, music, art, silence, and fellowship with other believers—have made a difference in you individually, as a couple, and in your marriage. How have you grown in grace through worship. List some of the blessings that the church has initiated in your life and in your marriage.

Closing Prayer

Dear God, our marriage and the opportunity to worship you are two of many blessings we have been given. Growing closer to you has helped us grow closer to each other. Thank you for the laughter as well as the quiet moments we have shared as a couple. Help us continue to grow together in faith toward you and more in love with each other. Amen.

12. God's Incredible Compliment

1. Don and Jean Shelby write that God invites us to be cocreators and offers us resources greater than our own upon which we can draw. They refer to this gift and promise as God's "incredible compliment." We are called to be cocreators of love, life, and marriage. What should be our response to this compliment? What responsibilities come with being a cocreator? What are the resources God provides that we can draw upon as cocreators?

2. The authors ask you to consider the cost of a vital and strong religious faith. The cost is the ongoing struggle to claim it, to keep it, and to share it. Discuss your own struggle and the price you have paid to maintain a strong faith. How has your spouse helped you grow in faith? What has been your strongest challenge? How has God helped you in your struggle?

3. When a couple get married, they expect their union will be successful. What many couples do not realize is that their love is not an instant ticket to a perfect marriage. The authors point out that people learn to love each other and that this is a process. Elements of this process include experiences, misunderstandings, joyful occasions, conflicts, disappointments, forgiveness, acceptance, and all the situations that make up a life. Think about your marriage and experiences you have shared. What has encouraged you to love each other? What role has God played? And where do you think you are right now in this learning process?

4. Love is vital to a successful marriage, but what is love? Love consists of promises kept, commitments made, mutual needs, trust, and reciprocity, among other things. In your own words, explain what love means to you and why you love your spouse. What keeps your love alive?

5. The writer Kathleen Norris is quoted in this essay that "intimacy is what *makes* a marriage." Explain what she means and if you agree. How do a couple grow in intimacy? What struggles are involved? Do you agree with her statement that "true intimacy is frightening"? Explain.

Reflection Question

6. Take some time to reflect on how you have responded to God's incredible compliment. Conduct a personal inventory and evaluation, focusing on the blessings and opportunities you have been given. Make a list of what you have created together through your marriage. Consider what other potential creations await you and your spouse.

Closing Prayer

Dear God, you've given all of us an incredible compliment by inviting us to be cocreators of life, love, and marriage. You have blessed us, encouraged us, and given us unconditional love. Thank you for all you have given us. May we share our love and our bounty with others. Amen.

13. Reflections on Marriage and the Spiritual Journey

1. The Hunts discuss how marriage led them to a deeper and enriched faith. They say that marriage is a metaphor that dramatizes God's love to humans. How has marriage deepened your faith? In what ways is your relationship with God similar to your relationship with your spouse?

2. How easy has it been to take your spouse's perspective? Has this grown easier over the years? How often have you discovered that you both have similar feelings? How do you meet the challenge of reaching out to the other in love rather than focusing on your own needs? How do God and your faith assist you in communicating your wants and needs?

3. The authors have found that each stage of life elicits its special perspective on God, making a circle of life. What are the different perspectives from childhood, to young adult, to newlyweds, to being a married couple with children. What causes you to gain a new perspective with each stage? What is the biggest change in perspective from being single to being a couple? What do you anticipate your perspective will be near the end of your life?

4. The Hunts strongly encourage couples to put God first in their marriage. What are the benefits of doing this? What motivates a couple to make this change? How does this alter a marriage? How does this change your viewpoint on disappointments and conflicts? What has been your experience in turning your marriage over to God?

5. In the ideal marriage, a couple grow in love and learn to stay together out of free choice. Conflicts and disappointments are overcome through love, understanding, and acceptance. Yet many marriages, even Christian marriages, end in divorce. How have you avoided divorce and maintained a loving relationship? Do you see any acceptable reasons for divorce?

Reflection Question

6. We begin with God, and we end with God. Take some time to reflect on your marriage and spiritual journey so far. Conduct an inventory of your life today. Write down some thoughts, ideas, wishes, hopes, and dreams as they come to you. Think of where you have traveled on your journey and where you want to go from here. Consider your future together.

Closing Prayer

Dear God, you have blessed us. You have helped us grow in wisdom and in love toward each other. We have learned more about each other and have a better understanding of what unconditional love really is. Thank you for guiding us in our marriage and on our spiritual journey. Continue to show us the paths you desire us to take as we walk in your ways. Amen.

14. Marriage as Sacrament and Covenant

1. In your own words, explain what covenant means to you in relationship to God and your marriage. What are the terms of your marriage covenant? Can a healthy relationship exist without a covenant? Does a covenant ever change? Explain.

2. The sacrament of marriage is modeled on Christ's covenant of love for the church, according to Ephesians 5:32. In your own words, explain what sacrament means to you in relationship to God and your marriage.

3. Compare and contrast your courtship and marriage ceremony to that of the authors. What feelings and special moments did you share? Were any rituals similar?

4. After the marriage ceremony, the authors felt God's presence and blessing. During what times of your relationship did you feel God was with you? Explain how you knew God was present. How did it make you feel?

5. How have social issues played a part in your marriage and relationship? Have they united or divided you? Has your involvement in social issues changed over the years? How does it affect your marriage and your relationship?

Reflection Question

6. Reflect on the importance of candor and sensitivity in a marriage. What lessons have you learned along the way? How can candor and sensitivity be balanced? What have you learned about honesty in your relationship to your spouse and to God?

Closing Prayer

Dear God, we have learned many things through our relationship and marriage, but we have so much more to learn. Help us remember the importance of hope, forgiveness, and patience toward each other and others. Thank you for your many blessings and the discoveries we continue to make about you, ourselves, others, and life. Be with us this coming week. Amen.

15. Happily Uncharted

1. Explain the meaning of the essay's title, "Happily Uncharted." What impressed or challenged you from the experiences shared by the authors? What experiences and feelings could you relate to? In what ways has your spiritual journey been uncharted?

2. Much of our spiritual growth comes from our experiences with others, knowledge shared, and travels to new places. What experiences or travels have influenced your spiritual life? Recall some of the people you have met on your travels who have influenced your spiritual life. How have these experiences strengthened your marriage and relationship with God?

3. The authors talk of their spiritual dialogue with others during their travels. Why is this dialogue so valuable? How has your spiritual dialogue influenced your faith and your marriage?

4. Has your spiritual journey given you knowledge and insights into other religions, cultures, and denominations? Explain. How has this knowledge been helpful in your spiritual development?

5. How have your travels and experiences opened your eyes about God's creation? What have you gained from some of the friends you have made during your journey? Have you gained a new perspective about human rights and social issues? Explain.

Reflection Question

6. The authors note how people often have limited perceptions that prevent them from embracing and enjoying God's full creation. Reflect on how your perception of others may be limited, and consider ways you can expand your world and knowledge. Think about how you can celebrate the differences in people. How can you use your marriage to broaden your world?

Closing Prayer

Dear God, our world is often so small, limited by our mind, our experiences, our attitudes, and our prejudices. Help us see the bigger picture and enjoy your full creation. May we celebrate the differences in others and look for what we have in common with different cultures and races. Bless our marriage as we continue our spiritual journey. Amen.

16. Marriage as a Spiritual Path

1. Share your insights and ideas about the quotation from Dostoevsky: "The person who desires to see the Living God face to face must not seek God in the empty firmament of the mind, but in human love." What is he saying about God and about love?

2. The authors share that at one point in their marriage, they lost the habit of approaching life from a Jesus perspective. Has this ever happened in your marriage? What causes this to happen?

3. After considering divorce, the authors decided to try to reconnect with the spiritual dimension of their lives and to experience the Living God working in their lives. They opened themselves to the possibility that faith could heal their broken relationship. How do you think this action helped their marriage and relationship? What is needed in order for faith to produce healing?

4. Have you ever reflected on "what God would want you to do" in order to reach a decision or find direction in your life or marriage? Explain the situation and how it was resolved.

5. What challenged or impressed you about the journey experienced by this couple? What experiences and feelings could you relate to? What truths have you discovered during times of trial in your marriage? Explain.

Reflection Question

6. Reflect on what you have learned from reading these sixteen essays. How has your relationship to your spouse and to God been changed by discussing this book? What essay had the greatest impact? What new insights did you gain?

Closing Prayer

Dear God, we thank you for this time together. Thank you for the honesty of the discussions and for being able to draw closer to you and each other. Bless all the couples who contributed to this book and shared their insights and experiences. Be with us as we continue this journey of faith. Amen.